At Issue

Is Society Becoming Less Civil?

Other Books in the At Issue Series:

At Issue

Is Society Becoming Less Civil?

Louise I. Gerdes, Book Editor

GREENHAVEN PRESS

A part of Gale, Cengage Learning

GALE
CENGAGE Learning·

Farmington Hills, Mich • San Francisco • New York • Waterville, Maine
Meriden, Conn • Mason, Ohio • Chicago

GALE
CENGAGE Learning·

Elizabeth Des Chenes, *Director, Content Strategy*
Douglas Dentino, *Manager, New Product*

© 2014 Greenhaven Press, a part of Gale, Cengage Learning

WCN: 01-100-101

BJ
/533
.C9
I82
2014

LIBRARY OF CONGRESS CATALOGING-IN-PUBLICATION DATA

Is society becoming less civil? / Louise I. Gerdes, book editor.
    pages cm. -- (At issue)
    Includes bibliographical references and index.
    ISBN 978-0-7377-6840-4 (hardcover) -- ISBN 978-0-7377-6841-1 (pbk.)
    1. Courtesy--Social aspects. 2. Courtesy--Political aspects. 3. Social interaction. I. Gerdes, Louise I., 1953-
    BJ1533.C9I82 2014
    302--dc23
                                                                    2014013001

Printed in the United States of America
1 2 3 4 5 6 7 18 17 16 15 14

Contents

Introduction

Frustrated drivers making obscene gestures, salespeople ignoring customers, cell phone users sharing intimate details of their private lives publicly in one-sided phone conversations, students texting or surfing the Internet during class, anonymous online commenters hurling racist insults—these are some of the uncivil behaviors in recent years that concern some observers. Even traditionally civil platforms are no longer immune to incivility: when country music star Taylor Swift is accepting a music award, hip hop artist Kanye West jumps on stage claiming that another singer was more deserving, and US congressman Joe Wilson of South Carolina shouts, "You lie!" during President Barack Obama's address to Congress in 2009, an unprecedented outburst. Some believe that this rudeness is a growing problem while others claim that incivility is nothing new—modern technology and media, they reason, simply make it appear more frequent. Whether the problem is a growing one or a phenomenon made more visible with the development of technology and media attention, some fear the impact of incivility, particularly in the political arena. Political lies and misrepresentations about political opponents and their views are one element of incivility of particular concern for some. Indeed, divergent views on the causes and impact of these flawed characterizations are reflective of the broader debate surrounding whether society is, in fact, less civil.

Throughout history, representatives of both parties have questioned the character of political opponents. During the 1964 presidential campaign, for example, then President Lyndon B. Johnson, a Democrat, ran an advertisement attacking his Republican opponent, Senator Barry Goldwater, on television that remains one of the most controversial political campaign ads. The ad shows a young girl counting petals on a daisy that dissolves into footage of a nuclear explosion backed by a voice counting down to zero. The goal of the ad was to imply that Goldwater was too hawkish to conduct foreign policy in an age of nuclear weapons. However, Republicans too have made unproven accusations. Some conservatives, for example, claim that President Barack Obama lied about being born in the United States. Although officials in Hawaii confirmed that Obama is indeed a native son, rumors nevertheless continue. Even the rhetoric responding to such claims is inflammatory. Indeed, liberal MSNBC commentator Chris Matthews asserts, "They know full well that he's American. They're out to destroy him personally. Yes, assassinate him with their lies."[1] Aspersions against political figures are, however, nothing new. In truth, opponents of Thomas Jefferson characterized him as "the son of a half-breed Indian squaw, sired by a Virginia mulatto father."[2] Nevertheless, some commentators claim that such characterizations are more common today and their impact more significant. According to Herbert W. Simons, professor of communications at Temple University in Philadelphia, "I don't recall any time when things were more problematic in terms of made-up factoids and innuendos and accusations that have no basis in truth."[3] For some, these uncivil rhetorical assaults in the political arena pose a serious threat.

One concern is the impact of uncivil misrepresentations in political discourse on the democratic process. Some analysts fear that when citizens are bombarded with lies and misrepresentations, they cannot effectively participate in the democratic process. According to Jennifer Jerit and Jason Barabas, associate professors of political science at Florida State University, "When elites provide information that is inaccurate, in-

---

1. Quoted in David Edwards, "Matthews: Birthers Trying to 'Assassinate' Obama with Lies," *The Raw Story* blog, August 5, 2010. http://www.rawstory.com/rs/2010/08/05/matthews-birthers-assassinate-obama-lies.
2. Joseph Cummins, *Anything for a Vote*. Philadelphia, PA: Quirk Books, 2007.
3. Quoted in Marcia Clemmitt, "Lies and Politics," *CQ Researcher*, February 18, 2011.

complete, or misleading, citizens may have mistaken evaluations of policy alternatives."[4] Moreover, concerned commentators maintain, public cynicism eats away at citizens' willingness to get involved in the political process. In fact, evidence shows that citizens do feel that political discourse leaves them uninformed. According to Clay Ramsay, director of research at the Program on International Policy Attitudes (PIPA), more than nine in ten voters said in 2011 that they received misleading information during the November 2010 election campaign, and 54 percent said that misinformation was greater than ever. In a democracy, policies are implemented through persuasion not force, these analysts assert. Indeed, some see political deception as a form of violence against citizens. According to Sissela Bok, a fellow at the Harvard School of Public Health and author of *Lying: Moral Choice in Public and Private Life*, lies and violence "are the two forms of deliberate assault on human beings."[5] Although political deception may to some appear relatively harmless, she paints a more discouraging picture. "Imagine a society, no matter how ideal in other respects, where word and gesture could never be counted upon. Questions asked, answers given, information exchanged—all would be worthless," Bok reasons.[6] In such a world, like-minded analysts argue, democracy cannot flourish. Unfortunately, concludes Wayne Fields, English professor at Washington University in St. Louis, Missouri, when truth and reason do not prevail, the nation risks "being destroyed as a democracy."[7]

Others assert, however, that innuendo, smears, half-truths, and outright lies are an inevitable part of the political process. They argue that the problem today is instead a decline in the ability of citizens to reason when faced with uncivil political

---

4. Jennifer Jerit and Jason Barabas, "Bankrupt Rhetoric: How Misleading Information Affects Knowledge About Social Security," *Public Opinion Quarterly*, Fall 2006.
5. Sissela Bok, *Lying: Moral Choice in Public and Private Life*. New York: Pantheon, 1978.
6. Ibid.
7. Quoted in Clemmitt, op. cit.

rhetoric. "I don't think lying is anything new," asserts J. Michael Hogan, codirector of the Center for Democratic Deliberation at Pennsylvania State University.[8] "As a historian of public discourse, I think the decline of reason is a bigger problem," he concludes.[9] Hogan claims, however, that journalists bear some of the blame for irrational political discourse. Indeed, like-minded communication experts maintain, the number of partisan television media outlets available make it difficult for people to separate facts from ideology. "You can pretty much dial up your own reality," claims University of Washington communication professor Lance Bennett.[10] Penn State's Hogan agrees, adding that today's journalists do less fact checking. Moreover, people are not likely to question information they receive from media outlets that share their ideology. "If you lie to somebody who disagrees with you, to their face, they'll call you on it. But if you lie in an echo chamber, you'll probably get away with it," Hogan reasons.[11] Nevertheless, research in political science, communication, and psychology reveal that nonpartisan media can do little to counteract lies and misrepresentations. "We tend to grab onto the very things we hear that fit into the biases we have already,"[12] says John Gastil, professor of communication at the University of Washington. He adds, "When I see something that sounds right to me, I accept it." Thus, Gastil concludes, "People who are politically oriented tend to become not just wrong but systematically wrong."[13]

Some observers express more optimism concerning the ability of the citizenry to participate in the democratic process when political discourse is rife with lies and misrepresentations. According to University of Kansas communications pro-

8. Ibid.
9. Ibid.
10. Ibid.
11. Ibid.
12. Ibid.
13. Ibid.

fessor Robert C. Rowland, while in the short term people may discount facts that contradict their philosophy, when these facts become regularly observable, the truth prevails and people abandon false beliefs. Even when attacked with lies, Rowland reasons, "over time the better argument does tend to win out."[14] He cites by way of example the ultimate granting of equal rights to minorities and women. Moreover, still others argue that voters ultimately make decisions based upon the reality that they face in their lives. Voters may sometimes make faulty decisions based on political deception, states Brendan Nyhan, Dartmouth College assistant professor of government and author of *All the President's Spin: George W. Bush, the Media and the Truth*. However, he counters, "there's not a ton of evidence that spin drives the political agenda."[15] Moreover, although sometimes a crisis is necessary, "Historically we know that politics tends to self-correct,"[16] claims Thomas Hollihan, a communications professor at the University of Southern California's Annenberg School for Communication and Journalism, particularly when those who use lies, rumors, and innuendo overreach. Historians cite the case of Senator Joseph McCarthy, who during the 1950s claimed that communists had infiltrated public and private US institutions. McCarthy "was an outrageous liar who knew he was lying and gleefully lied because it served his personal purposes,"[17] argues University of California, Davis, history professor Kathy Olmsted. However, McCarthy's lies were accepted when they helped his fellow Republicans. "But then he started telling lies about Republicans,"[18] Olmsted adds. This move ultimately led to a US Senate vote to condemn him, and McCarthy became a pariah—his peers left the Senate floor when he spoke.

14. Ibid.
15. Ibid.
16. Ibid.
17. Ibid.
18. Ibid.

Whether uncivil political rhetoric that misrepresents the character of political leaders and their views threatens the democratic process or is an inevitable and self-correcting part of the political process remains controversial. The authors in *At Issue: Is Society Becoming Less Civil?* debate these and other issues concerning a lack of civility in today's culture, its impact, and how best to address concerns. Whether incivility poses a significant threat to society remains to be seen.

1

Many Aspects of Society Are Less Civil

Paul Thoms

Paul Thoms, former choral director and district music supervisor for Fairfield City Schools in Ohio, served as a district office administrator working in curriculum and public relations. He speaks and writes on education and other topics and served as director of public relations for the Fitton Center for Creative Arts.

Although manners were once highly valued, many believe that Americans have in recent years become increasingly less civil in many areas of life. Some blame technology. Without the social barriers of face-to-face communication, people on the Internet, for example, feel free to be vulgar and rude. In addition, rude salespeople and disrespectful college students mimic the vulgar behavior they see on reality television. In politics, others claim, however, incivility is part of the democratic process. In truth, American history is rife with periods of political incivility. Nevertheless, civil debate on important issues is possible. Indeed, to function successfully as a community and counter growing self-centeredness, people must accept personal responsibility, cultivate empathy, and foster respect and kindness.

Until recently, almost everybody wanted to have good manners, which explains why books such as Emily Post's *Etiquette* were so popular in the last two centuries. They satisfied our middle-class anxieties, even though they *also* promoted snobbery. These books existed because they were needed: society had become more fluid, and people found themselves in unfamiliar situations, afraid they'd be embarrassed by saying the wrong thing, or using the wrong fork.

All that anxiety is gone today, and probably good riddance, because the message of old-fashioned manners books was: "People who are *better* than you know how to behave. Just follow their rules and you'll be okay."

Courtesy Among Other People

Well, manners *are* the traditions of a society that determine how we treat each other, and behave in public, but they're based on an ideal of empathy—of imagining the impact your actions have on others. They involve doing what you're not *obligated* to do, for the sake of other people. All the important rules boil down to this one: *remember who you are when you're with other people—show consideration.*

The word *courtesy* actually comes from the word *court.* The dictionary defines courteous as "marked by polished manners . . . marked by respect and consideration of others." To be courteous is to adopt the manners of the court, to treat one another like royalty.

When George Washington was a young man, he copied out a list of 110 *Rules of Civility and Decent Behavior in Company and Conversation.* One was, "Lean not upon anyone." Another was, "Read no letter, books or papers in company." And a third was, "If any one come to speak to you while you are sitting, stand up."

Washington's moral character set him apart, and he came to personify what you might call the dignity code, which lasted for decades, but, unhappily, hasn't survived to modern days.

In the past, we thought manners mattered; today, not so much. A number of surveys find that the great majority of us think Americans are becoming ruder. They also report that we're *concerned* about the incivility we see.

So, let's take a look at our present state of civility, both in general, and in more specific areas, such as politics, retail sales, on college campuses, and in technological communication. Later, we'll review some possible positive responses to the civility crisis.

It's as though some people have lost all sense of being out in public, or some inhibitor in their brain has been switched off.

The Present State of Civility

In 1932, Lady Astor's daughter was seen walking in Bond Street *without a hat on*, and people were shocked. Things have changed. Now we see bare midriffs, pierced navels, and visible underpants. Other societal shifts include technology-based communication, and open talk on topics which used to be taboo. The potential for awkward and rude moments has grown exponentially.

It's as though some people have lost all sense of being out in public, or some inhibitor in their brain has been switched off. People let doors swing into other people's faces, play loud music late at night, march into crowded elevators before anyone can get off, and litter with no sense of guilt. They're oblivious.

Rudeness in public is pervasive. You hear people on their cell phones describing their skin rash, drivers fail to use turn signals, people talk through a movie that you paid $9 to see, and still others refuse to obey directions from flight attendants.

The cover story of a recent issue of *USA Today* was titled, "Excuse Me, But ... Whatever Happened to Manners?" It discussed how impossible it is to ignore the growing rudeness in

American life. An overwhelming majority of Americans think incivility is a serious problem, and three in four said it's grown worse in the past decade, with the advent of email, cell phones and multi-tasking.

"Whatever happened to consideration?," we ask. Well, again, the prerequisite of consideration is the ability to imagine being in the other person's shoes, and that no longer happens consistently.

Parents have let their kids manipulate, insult and bully them. They've taught them to *demand* respect, but not to show it. And by doing this, they've failed the kids *and* they've failed the rest of us. And what about teaching by example. A recent survey reported that 71 per cent of Americans have seen parents at sports events "screaming" at coaches, referees, and players. And, have you noticed how *few* role models there are for respectfulness, and how *many* there are for rudeness, crassness, and nastiness?

Technology really does affect character. People say and do things in cyberspace that they wouldn't say and do face-to-face.

As today's generation grows older and travels around the world, people in other countries are often shocked by our informality and familiarity. My concern has to do with something more basic: the respect we owe one another. Without this, there isn't much point in talking about manners or etiquette.

Simply put, the neglect of courtesy leads to the collapse of community. The *heart* of courtesy is respect for others; it has less to do with manners than with how we relate to others.

Civility in Technological Communication

People have always associated new technologies with moral decline. In 1854, [Henry David] Thoreau griped, "Men think that it is essential that the Nation have commerce, and export ice, and talk through a telegraph, and ride thirty miles an hour . . . but whether we should live like baboons or like men, is a little uncertain."

Similar anxieties have greeted most inventions, from the automobile to the iPhone. Sometimes, though, the pessimists are right to worry. Technology really does affect character. People say and do things in cyberspace that they wouldn't say and do face-to-face.

It's natural to want to communicate, but being inconsiderate *is* a cause for concern, and we see it reflected in the fact that group pressure no longer seems to exist. In the past, a person might think; "I want to do this anti-social thing, but there are twenty other people here, so I won't." Now the response is: "I want to do this anti-social thing, and if anyone objects to it, tough!"

People who object to automated switchboards are dismissed as grumpy old technophobes, but it seems to me that modern customer relations are just rude.

Perhaps what has changed is media—primarily, the new media—the Internet, the blogosphere and everything from Facebook to Twitter. Because of this, even when we *do* communicate with people, we're less restrained because we don't have to deal with their reactions face-to-face. We tend to think of what happens online as not "really real," and that on the Net anything can be said about any topic, or anyone, at any time.

And isn't it confusing that our biggest experience of *formal* politeness comes from recorded messages which aren't really sincere—messages such as, "Your call is important to us," or "Thank you for choosing to wait for our next agent," as if you had a choice.

The *internet* seems to have doomed *grammar;* now *technology* seems to be contributing to the end of *manners.* Wherever you turn for help, you find you're on your own. You phone a company to ask a question and invariably you're connected to an automatic switchboard. Suddenly, in a huge transfer of effort, *you* have a lot of work to do. In the past, you'd tell an operator why you were calling, and they'd put you through to the right person. But, today, we all seem to have become employees of every company we contact.

Today, people who *object* to automated switchboards are dismissed as grumpy old technophobes, but it seems to me that modern customer relations are just rude, because switchboards don't even meet you halfway. Once again, manners are about imagination—about imagining the other person. *These* systems, where we navigate ourselves, are clearly for someone else's convenience.

We seem to live in electronic isolation, with no concern about developing social skills. The huge number of messages in cyberspace doesn't show that we *need* others; instead, it shows that we're hiding ourselves online. And that's one reason for our thoughtless conversations on the Internet. We may need others, but we want them to stay at a safe distance. We want to connect to them, but not at our door. The Internet has even changed the meaning of words such as *friend*.

Civility in Retail Service

The quality of retail service has also substantially declined in recent decades. Rudeness from salespeople has become a common occurrence. We used to notice when service was *bad*; now we notice when it's *good*.

Incivility in retail service is a vicious circle: poor service causes customers to behave rudely, and customer rudeness leads to poor service. *Breaking* the circle should be the goal for any of us who shop in stores, eat in restaurants, go to doctors, answer the telephone—in other words, *all* of us.

Certainly we can put some of the blame on television. The theme of most reality shows is abuse, and we constantly see people being vulgar and rude to each other in contrived reality shows that encourage competition, and self-interest. No wonder our expectations are getting lowered, and our attitude to other people is so casual.

Ninety-five percent of Americans say civility in politics is important for a healthy democracy.

Civility in Politics

Recent political events and trends, from out-of-control town-hall meetings to rants on television, to [US Representative] Joe Wilson's shout of "You lie," at President [Barack] Obama [in 2009], have brought on even more concern about civility in *government.*

President Obama addressed civility directly in a commencement address at [the University of] Notre Dame, where he said, "One of the things I'm trying to figure out is, how can we make sure that civility is interesting." But the question is "Do Americans really want to be civil?"

Some say our nostalgia for civility is exaggerated, because during the Andrew Jackson–John Quincy Adams election of 1828, the former general was called a murderer and a cannibal, and his wife was accused of being a harlot.

But, ninety-five percent of Americans say civility in politics *is* important for a healthy democracy. The poll also found that 87 percent of Americans think it's possible for us to disagree about politics respectfully, though nearly half say there's been a decline of civility in politics.

On the positive side: Each year, the Aspen Institute offers fellowships to a dozen Republicans and a dozen Democrats, and exposes them to deep thinking and civil discourse. Recently, Ohio state senators who had been Institute fellows say the program helped them be more civil and understanding.

During the fellowship, they read and discussed the writings of Plato, Martin Luther King, John Locke and other great thinkers.

Columnist David Brooks says it's not right to end on a note of cultural pessimism, because there is the fact of President Obama. Whatever policy differences people may have with him, most of us can probably agree that he exemplifies traits associated with dignity. Let's hope he can revitalize that concept for the next generation.

Civility on the College Campus

If we really want civility, we have to find a way to make it interesting to young people and begin teaching debating skills to high school and college students. Making debate cool is a challenge, partly because clear thinking is hard work and takes skill and discipline.

Some have called this an age of social autism, where people can't seem to see the impact their actions have on others, and always lay responsibility on the other person.

The question being raised, more and more, on college campuses, is, "Whatever happened to common courtesy, and what can we do about it?" There are plenty of examples of questionable behavior: The recent secret videotaping of a college freshman in a sexual encounter with another man, which was posted to *millions* on the internet, comes to mind.

The gay freshman, at Rutgers [State University of New Jersey], where he was videotaped, jumped to his death from a campus bridge, after the posting. The university is now involved in a two-year study called Project Civility. And, at George Mason University, they currently offer an elective called Professionalism and Civility. Their lecturer says, "People don't take the time to think about consequences."

The chancellor at the University of Wisconsin says a number of factors contribute to the ugliness, including the anonymity of technology; increased campus diversity; alcohol; and the political climate. He says we need to quit treating these things as if they're isolated events, so on campuses all across the country, civility is an issue of growing concern.

The interesting thing is that when we operate without a sense of responsibility or community, we're miserable, lonely, and rude. Some have called this an age of social autism, where people can't seem to see the impact their actions have on others, and always lay responsibility on the other person.

How to Deal with It

So, how do we deal with the rudeness we find all around us? First of all, we shouldn't personalize rude behavior. Even when it's *directed* at us, it's probably not *about* us, but as a result of sleep deprivation, depression, stress, illness, or insecurity. We should probably cool off and calm down. If we can, we might be able to keep the rudeness from escalating, because "An eye for an eye" isn't a good approach. We shouldn't respond to rudeness *with* rudeness.

One angry action can provoke another, until we find ourselves in a sorry mess. Violence never stops with those who deserve it, but bounces back with even more energy. When a stranger is rude, and you're tempted to strike back, instead take a moment to reflect. If you knew this person would you treat him rudely? Pretend that the stranger's an acquaintance and see how your attitude changes. You're probably less likely to be rude.

Also, we need to accept the *reality* of rudeness. No matter where you are, or what you're doing, rudeness can happen when you least expect it. So, expect it! Expect the car behind you in the next lane to speed up as soon as you signal that you're switching to that lane. Expect that in the grocery store parking lot one car will hog two spaces. Realizing that thoughtless behavior can and will happen, might save your sanity.

Be sensitive to those things that bother others. A survey on Yahoo resulted in the following concerns: discrimination on the job; aggressive driving; taking credit for someone else's work; treating service providers as inferiors; making jokes about race, gender, age, disability, sexual preference or religion; bullying; littering; misusing handicapped privileges; smoking in nonsmoking places; and using cell phones or texting during conversations or meetings.

College student scores on the Narcissistic Personality Inventory have increased by 30 percent since 1991.

In the end, always let empathy be your guide in understanding rudeness. Know how to respond, and when to leave the scene. When necessary, set limits, and if the conversation gets irrational, know when to quit. Acceptance of rudeness doesn't mean you're a wimp. You don't have to like what happened, but you can come to terms with it. . . .

More Self-Absorbed, Less Empathetic

Are we too self-involved? Today, immodesty *does* seem to be everywhere. There's [hip hop artist] Kanye West grabbing the microphone from [country music star] Taylor Swift at the MTV Awards to tell us that the wrong person won. And baseball and football games are now so often interrupted by self-celebration that we don't even notice it anymore.

Studies suggest that we *have* become more self-absorbed. College student scores on the Narcissistic Personality Inventory have increased by 30 percent since 1991. This is reflected in the fact that self-centeredness is at the heart of discourtesy. We're back to the issue of control—I want *my* will and *my* desires to be served; I want people to fit into *my* plans.

The idea that modern America is in a state of self-regard dates to the 1970s when writers like Tom Wolfe critiqued what he dubbed the "me decade." But the research suggests that American self-involvement is actually reaching a new high in this age of Facebook and Twitter. According to sociologists, younger Americans are more self-absorbed and less empathetic than earlier generations—and the trend seems to have accelerated as our Internet culture has grown.

Whatever we want, we want it now. The remote control is a reminder of our shrinking attention span and our pursuit of instant gratification.

The neglect of timely RSVPs falls into this category. Self-centeredness makes us insensitive to another person's needs to plan and make preparations. If I don't take time to communicate my intentions, it's because I don't want to be bothered with an interruption in *my* plans for *my* day in *my* life.

Rudeness needs to be addressed, because it can accelerate. A person who flips off the bird when cut off in traffic is more apt to spit in the face of an umpire and, maybe even aim a gun at another person guilty of being the wrong race, nationality or religion.

Drawing Conclusions

So, what can we conclude about our look at civility? Well, I think we can say that bad manners can hurt feelings and relationships. They determine how happy we are, how long we live, and they help us find our place in the world and our reason for being here.

As P.M. Forni, author of *The Civility Solution*, says, "Most Americans blame rudeness on people leading busier lives and not taking time for politeness. We fast-forward, speed-dial, FedEx, speed-date, and dashboard-dine. We face deadlines, channel-surf, and instant-message. . . . We run all day, and at night we relax with a fast-paced novel. Whatever we want, we want it now. The remote control is a reminder of our shrinking attention span and our pursuit of instant gratification."

Being too busy *does* prevent us from controlling our lives; it causes stress, makes people sick, causes accidents, makes otherwise polite people rude, and reduces our general level of happiness.

We're so consumed with our *personal* race that we don't take the time to notice the world around us. Kindness takes time and we don't seem to have it, but *if* we slow down, our stress levels go down, and we begin to value others more, and behave with more consideration.

Rudeness *begets* rudeness just as politeness begets politeness so responding in kind makes it more difficult to change another person's attitude, and adding rudeness to rudeness gets in the way of any healing process.

Feeling empathy for strangers is good for us; it makes us feel better about ourselves, and encourages us to be better people *and*, it's contagious. We all *want* respect, approval, praise, and kindness. In return, we should always *grant* these to others—generously and sincerely.

We need to remember that our quality of life depends on our willingness to control our own needs and wants. Restraint makes civilized life possible. In the past, good manners were seen as important, and restraint was second nature; we need to encourage a return to those values.

2

Bleep! The Decline of Civility

Kathleen Parker

Kathleen Parker is a nationally syndicated columnist who in addition to The Washington Post, *has contributed to* The Weekly Standard, Time, *and* USA Today. *Parker is also a frequent guest on NBC's* The Chris Matthews Show.

Despite ubiquitous media images of incivility, Americans are not less civil than in times past. Indeed, Americans have always been boisterous and unrestrained. Although the rules of decorum may have loosened in recent years, the call to improve our behavior is as old as American incivility itself. Nevertheless, deteriorating manners have in fact crept into public discourse. However, blaming the media is unfair, as people find passionate argument more entertaining than calm debate. In the end, most Americans would prefer public incivility over restrictions on speech. The best way to counter incivility is for good people to act according to their conscience and for the media to avoid giving undue attention to flawed thinking.

Can civility be saved?

This has become the question du jour [of the day] among scholars, journalists and others who fret about such things at dozens of programs popping up around the country. As a nation, we seem to want to be a more civil society, which is laudable if, quite possibly, unlikely.

An Historical Concern About Incivility

Inevitably, discussions about the current state of civility begin with disclaimers and acknowledgment that Americans have always been a bunch of rowdies and rascals. Previous eras have made current incivility look like a (real) tea party that erupts into a food fight of crumpets and scones.

A perennial favorite was the caning administered by South Carolina Rep. Preston Brooks upon the person of Massachusetts Sen. Charles Sumner over a disagreement about slavery and a question of honor. And, of course, there was that little episode known as the Civil War.

Are we less civil today than in the past? Not really, though thanks to the pervasiveness of media, it seems that way. And, thanks to the general coarsening of the culture amid the breakdown of traditional institutions, not to mention families, rules of decorum have suffered.

Even the imperative to improve the tone of our interactions is a constant through history. Sometime around age 16, George Washington transcribed a slim volume called "Rules of Civility & Decent Behaviour in Company and Conversation," which covered everything from when and how to spit to how to speak in public. The 58th rule reads:

Behaviors once associated with rougher segments of society have become mainstream.

"Let your Conversation be without Malice or Envy, for 'tis a Sign of a Tractable and Commendable Nature: And in all Causes of Passion admit Reason to Govern."

Ahem, yes, well, tell that to a certain member of Congress from South Carolina. We should all write Joe "You lie!" Wilson [who shouted "You lie!" during President Barack Obama's address to Congress in 2009] a thank-you note for creating a contemporary standard by which to judge public expressions of incivility. We might also stamp a letter to the congresswoman from California, Maxine Waters, who recently described House Republican leaders as "demons."

The Perception of the Beholder

Like so many things, civility is in the perception of the beholder, but we at least can agree on a definition. Civility is courtesy in behavior and speech, otherwise known as manners. In the context of the public square, civility is manners for democracy.

Unquestionably, our manners have deteriorated since Washington's time, increasingly so in recent years. Manners have become quaint, while behaviors once associated with rougher segments of society have become mainstream.

During my childhood, even private cursing was rare, and the third finger was something only the crudest people used to express themselves. No one I knew ever dropped the F-bomb. The worst children heard was an occasional "hell" or "damn," usually following an incident involving a badly aimed hammer.

Better that incivility be revealed in the light of day than that it be forced underground, there to fester and the underlying sentiments to grow.

Given that manners have faded in our interpersonal relations, it shouldn't be surprising that bad habits would bleed into the public square. Add to the equation our social media, Internet access and other avenues of instant and, importantly, anonymous, communication, and the bad habits of the few become the social pathology of the many. As we further balkanize ourselves, finding comfort in virtual salons of ideological conformity, it becomes easier to dehumanize "the other" and treat him accordingly.

How to Address Bad Manners

Whom to blame and how to fix it? It is tempting to blame "the media," especially television, for the degradation of civility. Obviously the food-fight formula that attracts viewers to cable TV isn't helpful, but we may protest too much. We can always change the channel, but people arguing passionately are more entertaining than solemn folks speaking in measured tones about Very Important Issues. Conflict and spectacle sell (see WWE [World Wrestling Entertainment] and its distant ancestor, the Colosseum). The attraction is tied to our sporting spirit and the lure of the contest.

The clearest solution would be unacceptable to most of us. That is, the tamping down of speech. Better that incivility be revealed in the light of day than that it be forced underground, there to fester and the underlying sentiments to grow. Change—if we really want it—has to come from within, each according to his own conscience.

The most that media can do, meanwhile, is strive to be honest, accurate and fair, and reward the coarsest among us with scant attention. The greatest threat to civility isn't the random "You lie!" outburst. More threatening to our firmament is the pandering to ignorance, the elevation of nonsense and the distribution of false information.

In the main, the Golden Rule works pretty well. Best taught in the home, it could use some burnishing.

3

Society Seems to Be Crossing a Line of Civility

Rich Heldenfels, Beacon Journal popular culture writer

Rich Heldenfels writes on culture issues for the Akron Beacon Journal, *an Ohio newspaper.*

Concerns about growing incivility in American politics are unwarranted. American politics has, in fact, always lacked civility. For example, an academic of the day claimed that the election of Thomas Jefferson would lead to Bible burning. Indeed, some claim that the controversial inflammatory commentary of radio talk show host Rush Limbaugh is mild compared to Father Coughlin, a 1930s radio talk show host that some call the father of hate radio. In truth, the media may make incivility appear more commonplace. In the past, television had few networks and none saw incivility as newsworthy. Today, however, many competing networks see incivility as news and air it repeatedly. Nevertheless, media self-policing can mediate concerns that images of incivility breed more incivility.

Or Maybe Technology Just Makes Rudeness Appear More Pervasive

When Republican Rick Santorum calls President Obama a "snob," has some line of civility been crossed? When Democrat Maxine Waters calls Republican leaders in Congress "demons," has that same line been crossed from the other political side? And what does that mean to political discourse generally?

What about the anonymous commenter on Ohio.com who called another commenter a "dumb a$$"? Or the one who called a *Beacon Journal* columnist "a bully and self serving bozo"? (This is not the last time you will see "bozo" in this story.) Or the commenter who blasted "a bribed, stupid, gluttonous, obese, and corrupt moron."

While some comments are deleted from Ohio.com for being inappropriate, none of those had been as of Thursday.

When political provocateur Andrew Breitbart died last week and received many respectful eulogies, more than one noted that Breitbart had called Ted Kennedy a "duplicitous bastard" and other epithets when the Massachusetts senator died. Breitbart in turn was called "a traitor" by one critic commenting on his death.

It seems, at times, that civility has absented the public conversation, especially about social issues, particularly in politics. A sitting president can be called a liar in the middle of his State of the Union Address. A commentator can call Republican ideas the province of "fools and clowns."

With all the problems and worries facing people every day, polite interaction may no longer seem to yield solutions. After all, we are a nation that has seen all kinds of content get more graphic and blunt, including in movies and on television. Twenty years ago, a TV show shocked some critics by having a little girl tell another character, "You suck." These days, that would raise no eyebrows in network executive suites.

But when opinions are plainly and unbendingly expressed, there appears to be no point in trying to bridge divides. A successful attempt seems a novelty.

When the Humane Society of the United States was at odds with egg producers, the producers' rep asked, "Why would you want to have a conversation with someone who wants to eliminate your business?" And when both sides actually began talking and figured out a legislative compromise, an NPR report called their understanding "unconventional"— and wondered "whether Congress will find that appealing or suspect."

Common ground is unconventional? Compromise could be suspect?

It makes one wonder what was said by the NPR.org commenters who weighed in on the egg story and found their comments deleted because they "did not meet the NPR.org Community Discussion Rules."

Bozos and Pink Underwear

All the flying invective could be bad news.

"Both participants and observers of national politics believe that disrespectful and discourteous behavior is inhibiting the solution of pressing national problems," says the report of the Ohio Civility Project.

The recent vitriol in Congress pales next to some previous eras.

"When people engage in (uncivil behavior), the other side responds in kind," said Kathleen Hall Jamieson, a professor at the Annenberg School for Communication who is a nationally known expert on politics and author of *Dirty Politics*. "As a result you've lost the ability to engage in argument."

Only, when did we lose it—if we in fact lost it at all?

Consider this:

- A politician, trying to explain the Communist (or red) leanings of an opponent, proclaimed her "pink right down to her underwear."

- Another politician looked at his opposition and said his dog knew more about foreign affairs than those "bozos."

- A distinguished academic once claimed that a presidential contender's election would lead to the Bible being burned.

The underwear comment dates to 1950, the "bozos" remark to 1992. And the Bible threat was laid on Thomas Jefferson more than 200 years ago.

Americans Are Rowdy

For all that is said about the decline of civility, Americans are of rowdy stock, and politics has not been patty-cake. In a telephone interview, Jamieson said that the recent vitriol in Congress pales next to some previous eras.

A 2011 report on Civility in Congress by the Annenberg Public Policy Center of the University of Pennsylvania looked at one barometer: How often the words of House of Representatives members were removed from the Congressional Record for violating its elaborate rules for civility. (As the report notes, the rules warn against calling another member a liar "even if he or she is not telling the truth.") By that measure, the two years that stand out between 1935 and 2010 are 1995, when the so-called Republican revolution swept into the House, and 1946, when, Jamieson said, fears about Communism led to "very, very strident" rhetoric.

Radio personality Rush Limbaugh has often been held up as the embodiment of rough talk, and he was in the news again lately when he applied the words "slut" and "prostitute" to a college student who had called for employers to include contraception in their health care. But Limbaugh would look tame compared to Father Coughlin, Jamieson said, referring to the 1930s radio preacher sometimes called "the father of hate radio."

There may still be rhetorical lines that commentators cross at their peril. Jamieson noted that neither Glenn Beck on the right nor Keith Olbermann on the left now has a major TV bullhorn, Beck having left Fox News while Olbermann departed MSNBC (although he is now on the smaller Current TV).

"You don't give up people making large amounts of money unless there's some kind of push-back that will hurt your brand," she said.

Jamieson, a co-founder of the politician-scrutinizing FactCheck.org website, in January launched FlackCheck.org, a site that looks in various ways at the rhetorical excesses and deceptions in public debate. (The Santorum and Waters comments beginning this story, for example, are both showcased on the site.)

We had (incivility) out there all along, but it wasn't newsworthy enough to get into the network nightly news.

"We're posting everything we can find," she said, and the site takes pains to match excessive language from one side with comparable remarks from the other. "If (incivility) really was the dominant thing in discourse, wouldn't we have hundreds of items a day? Maybe we're getting two a week, three a week. And we're really looking for it."

Media Make It Worse

But what is happening, Jamieson suspects, is that the media landscape has made it seem that incivility is pervasive by showcasing even the smallest examples nonstop on 24-hour news channels and the Internet.

"When something occurs once, you will hear about it many, many more times than you ever would when we only had three major news networks and they only aired a half-hour of nightly news," she said. "My suspicion is that we had (incivility) out there all along, but it wasn't newsworthy enough to get into the network nightly news. Now it not only gets in, but its availability is increased dramatically because it's played again and again, so you overestimate how much there is."

And how you judge the relative civility of different parties can depend on where you get your information.

"We're going to release a study in about two weeks . . . that shows that if you listen and watch MSNBC a lot, and you don't watch Fox, you will think, based on what you see, that it's conservatives who are uncivil all the time," Jamieson said. "And if you watch Fox a lot, and don't watch MSNBC, it's the liberals you will think are uncivil all the time. And if you watch CNN all the time, you'll think both sides are uncivil— and there's more incivility, because you see it on both sides."

Then if the assumption becomes that everyone is uncivil, that could indeed lead to more incivility because that's how everyone believes a debate should go.

So is it possible to find reasoned solutions amid the noise and insults?

The Ohio Civility Project's recommendations include "setting the standards for the appropriate tone of public discourse, and providing information about how well the major players live up to these standards."

Jamieson also argues that the supporters of a given cause or candidate have to police themselves. Some of that appeared to be happening with Limbaugh's comments, when the chorus of critics included House Speaker John Boehner, a Limbaugh ally, who said through a spokesman that Limbaugh's choice of words was "inappropriate."

"That's what makes the system work," she said. "The system doesn't work because the other side is policing you; you're not paying any attention to them." That also means that, if one side admits error, the other side (and its associated media) has to note it. Too often, she said, "all the other side covers is the outrageous thing, and not the apology."

So she looks at something like her websites "to try to get the decibel level dropped enough that people can see the legitimate differences between the candidates, between the parties. If that doesn't happen, then people just vote their ideologies—and the independents, who aren't guided by a strong ideology, are just confused. And the danger is that they're turned off and they don't vote at all. And that's not good."

4

Incivility Does Not Reflect a Breakdown in Democratic Society

Tod Lindberg

Tod Lindberg, a research fellow at the Hoover Institution and a member of its task force on the Virtue of a Free Society, is former editor of Policy Review, *a conservative publication that ceased publication in March 2013.*

Political incivility has a long history in the United States and often rises during periods when opposing parties feel strongly about contemporary issues. Incivility in public debate does not, however, reflect a breakdown in society but instead the nation's commitment to freedom of speech and democracy. Moreover, while discussion of politics may be uncivil, decorum remains in places where it matters most—where people make political decisions. Thus, debate on the congressional floor and in the courtroom is measured, and the law prohibits efforts to influence voters at the polling booth. Indeed, the nation's commitment to free speech is so strong that it criminalizes only public speech that would incite violence. In truth, the appearance of increased political incivility may simply be due to the fact that Americans have more platforms available to freely express their views.

"Bush lied, People Died," said the post-Iraq [war] bumper sticker. "You lie!" shouted Rep. Joe Wilson at President [Barack] Obama during a 2009 speech to a joint session of

Tod Lindberg, "The Politics of Incivility," *Commentary*, September 1992. Reprinted from COMMENTARY, September 1992, by permission; copyright © 1992 by Commentary, Inc.

Congress. The two examples constitute, respectively, Exhibit A for the GOP [Republican party] lament of the decline of civility in American life and Exhibit A for the same lament from the Democratic side.

A Long Pedigree

Despite what you have been hearing lately, incivility is nothing new in American politics. As Daniel M. Shea and Morris P. Fiorina note in their new edited volume *Can We Talk? The Rise of Rude, Nasty, Stubborn Politics,* incivility has a long pedigree in American political discourse. Consider the warning the *Connecticut Courant* issued about the consequences of a Thomas Jefferson victory in the presidential election of 1800: "Murder, robbery, rape, adultery and incest will be openly taught and practiced. . . . The soil will be soaked with blood." Or the taunt in 1884 arising from allegations that Grover Cleveland had had an affair with a young widow and fathered an illegitimate child: "Ma, Ma, where is Pa? Gone to the White House, Ha! Ha! Ha!"

Nevertheless, it is hard to spend much time on political websites these days without finding somebody calling somebody else a "douchebag" or an "ass-hat." Writing in the *American Journal of Political Science* in January 2007, Deborah Jordan Brooks and John G. Geer propose an operational definition of incivility as "claims that are inflammatory and superfluous." The "douchebag" proliferation certainly fits.

> *Incivility may be a defect, but the conditions that give rise to it have their virtues as well.*

It may be that incivility in politics has a cyclical character, perhaps associated with times when the contending parties feel the stakes are especially high, as they seem to feel now. No doubt, as Fiorina notes, "the sorting of politically active Americans into parties that have grown much more homogeneous than they were in the mid-20th century" has been a contributor to incivility, as people encounter fewer fellow partisans with significantly different positions on issues. Moreover, the ubiquity of cellphone cameras and the profusion of social media mean that "rude, nasty politics is dragged into our homes and into our daily lives with or without our consent," as Shea and Fiorina write. "Again, the tone of politics might be no rougher than in past eras, but we simply are exposed to more of it."

Americans themselves, in numerous public opinion surveys, believe that incivility is on the rise. In a poll of registered voters for the Center for Political Participation at Allegheny College in November 2010, days before the congressional elections that gave the GOP control of the House, 63 percent of respondents said politics had become "less civil" since Obama became president. In an August 2011 Rasmussen Reports survey, 76 percent of respondents expressed the view that Americans are becoming "more rude, less civilized." Whether American politics is newly uncivil or conditions have arisen in which our inner incivility is finally finding an outlet, nowadays, when people dish, the dish is louche.

Yet to lament the decline in civility, and leave it at that, is to miss several important elements of the contemporary American experience. Incivility may be a defect, but the conditions that give rise to it have their virtues as well: a robust tradition of freedom of expression, an energetic commitment to democratic self-government and the partisan wrangling that goes along with it, and a new political culture in which the barriers to entry into debate have never been lower and the ability to attract an audience never greater.

In addition, there is the remarkable fact that American politics remains civil where it matters the most. Talk about politics is raucous and rude, but the practice of debating and passing legislation, governing, and adjudicating remains measured, sober, and deliberative. We are not so far gone as we sometimes like to think. And as for those who decry incivility—often, in their denunciations, falling prey to it themselves—how often is lack of civility the problem, and how often is the problem that people with whom they disagree simply won't shut up?

The Consequences of Incivility

"An armed society is a polite society," pronounced the science-fiction writer Robert A. Heinlein in his novel *Beyond This Horizon*. His provocation has been especially popular among gun-rights enthusiasts. The idea seems to be that if the consequences for outrageous or even merely rude behavior toward another person could be lethal, people will treat each other in a civil and respectful manner.

Though it runs deeply counter to the conventional progressive American view, which holds that the proliferation of guns is dangerous, the Heinlein aphorism has an intuitive appeal: Would you mouth off at someone who has a six-shooter holstered to his belt? Probably you would think twice. Would you, the pedestrian crossing the road at the crosswalk with the light, give the finger to the turning car that failed to yield to you, if the odds were that the driver had a handgun and was ready to use it to pay you back for your rude gesture? Maybe not.

A society in which powerful social sanction extends beyond private speech to public *speech will be more "polite" . . . than a society in which public speech is governed only by the rules and rights of a liberal political and legal regime.*

Heinlein clearly approves of the armed utopia he has devised and the manly, ready-to-draw civility that comes with it. His epigram, however, is worth consideration not only in the form in which he proffers it, but perhaps even more so in its logically equivalent contrapositive form: "If a society is *not* polite, then it *must not* be armed."

Unless civility is somehow a natural condition of human interaction, which would seem to run counter to both [evolutionist Charles] Darwin *and* the Bible (not to mention Heinlein), then conditions of civility must come about either because people have a positive motive to be civil to one another, or have some cause to fear the consequences of the failure to treat one another civilly. Those negative consequences could take any number of forms: You might be challenged to a duel for behaving rudely, or get slapped in the brig, or find yourself ostracized by your social group.

It matters enormously whether the consequences are of an *official* or a *private* character. Private speech is subject to social, not political or legal, sanction. If one is abusive toward associates, they may be inclined to dissolve the association (though within the family, it's more complicated, as it is when the abusive person enjoys a power advantage in the relationship). One may not say just anything one pleases with impunity: Social sanction for uncivil behavior, while it does not deprive one of life or liberty, can be painful to the psyche. In private speech, there is an incentive among friends and associates to maintain civility; everyone is in a sense "armed" with the ability to participate in sanctioning bad behavior. Indeed, although private speech has certainly grown coarser and sailors curse no more flamboyantly than anybody else these days, there's no indication that the civility of private speech has declined at all.

A society in which powerful social sanction extends beyond private speech to *public* speech will be more "polite"— i.e., conformist with regard to social norms for behavior— than a society in which public speech is governed only by the rules and rights of a liberal political and legal regime. This may help explain why political discourse in certain other modern liberal states has not become as unruly as ours.

Fighting Words

Still, it is an entirely different phenomenon when rudeness is something determined under color of authority, and when sanctions for rudeness have the force of law. For the state to deprive a person of life, liberty, or property for the crime of incivility, rudeness, or disrespect directed toward those in authority—or those upon whom the authorities smile—is a far more serious proposition.

> *The rigorous constitutional protections for freedom of speech in the United States . . . mean that one may make outrageous comments about even the highest of public officials without fearing loss of liberty.*

And it is rare. In the 1942 case *Chaplinsky v. New Hampshire*, the U.S. Supreme Court held that certain kinds of speech were not subject to the protection of the First Amendment (and therefore could be prohibited by the state). Included were "fighting words," defined by the Court as "those that by their very utterance inflict injury or tend to incite an immediate breach of the peace." Since then, however, the Court has significantly narrowed its view of what the state might prohibit on the grounds of "fighting words."

Meanwhile, the idea of "fighting words" in the colloquial sense of a justification for coming out swinging is in grave disrepute, as James Bowman notes in his book *Honor: A History*. If someone attacks you physically, you have the right to defend yourself by force. But there really is no longer any category of *verbal* provocation held to justify a violent response. An offense against one's "honor" does not excuse violent reprisal. Dueling is illegal even if consensual. Although people sometimes still fight, including over honor, from the schoolyard to the barroom to the 'hood, they do so without legal permission or the blessing of polite society, which holds that resorting to force is off-limits. If someone directs "fighting words" at you and you, in your ensuing rage, kill him, you might at best face a second-rather than first-degree murder charge. So it doesn't matter what people say about you *or* your mother.

There are, of course, certain speech acts that still draw the attention of the authorities. You can rant and rave all you like, but if you threaten someone, you are asking for trouble. And if directed at (for example) the president of the United States, a rant giving indication of potentially dangerous mental disturbance, even though unaccompanied by a threat, will probably land the ranter on a Secret Service "watch" list. Note that it is not simply the uncivil speech that draws official scrutiny, but the intrusion of violence by way of discourse, even if the threat is empty or unserious or exists only in your potential to do harm to yourself or others.

Incivility in politics, on all sides, nowadays comes with a support group.

But these exceptions aside, the rigorous constitutional protections for freedom of speech in the United States and most other liberal societies mean that one may make outrageous comments about even the highest of public officials without fearing loss of liberty, much less loss of life. And as long as your incivility falls short of the stringent legal criteria for establishing slander or libel, your property is also secure from damage claims resulting from your speech.

Even though legal sanction for speech mostly doesn't exist in the United States, social sanctions do continue to have great effect in forestalling incivility. The question, then, is why there is less social sanction for incivility in "public speech" (that intended for a broad audience) than there used to be, as opposed to the ongoing social sanction that has kept "private speech" (that intended for one other person only or perhaps a small group) more civil.

The Public Nature of Political Speech

Political speech is by nature public, intended to be heard or read by others (even if the identity of the speaker or author is not necessarily meant to be known). The political conversation on today's Internet lies in a direct path from Speaker's Corner in London's Hyde Park. As with Speaker's Corner, the Internet is a place for wide-open debate. Both Speaker's Corner and the Web stand as symbols of a commitment to free speech. And both also, it happens, attract a substantial number of wild-eyed fanatics. It is especially political speech that has become uncivil today. That's because speakers no longer perceive politics itself and therefore political speech as a matter of life and death. Expressions of opinion and disagreement can be uncivil without dangerous consequences.

Public speech always has an element of performance. Speakers seek attention for themselves. They may find that the more inflammatory their remarks, the more effective they are in drawing an audience. This is not the only way to draw an audience, of course, but it's one way. Those most passionate about the views they hold may reward those who most passionately express the same view. In addition, incivility in politics, on all sides, nowadays comes with a support group. Your incivility, in addition to enraging your opponents, also pleases and galvanizes your friends, shoring up your side.

One-Sided Complaints

Complaints about incivility tend to be one-sided: One overlooks the incivility of one's friends to focus on the incivility of one's opponents. When a left-wing commentator denounces a conservative politician for incivility and demands that conservatives repudiate what the politician has said, liberals will tend to agree on the need for more civility. And vice versa. But this has little to do with a passion for civility and everything to do with partisan politics.

Genuinely nonpartisan calls for civility have a different constituency, perhaps of a mythical nature: the "broad middle" said to be turned off by the extreme rhetoric of both sides. But one must ask: Is it really high principle motivating this constituency? Or is this a group whose common characteristic is its indifference to politics as partisans of both sides practice it? If the latter, then it is not properly a "constituency" at all.

It is striking that nothing has come of the efforts to transform this "broad middle" into a majority voting bloc that could seize political control. If everyone falls somewhere on a continuum from left to right, then in principle one could win by commanding the 51 percent in the middle. But in practice, it hasn't worked. The most likely reason is that the "continuum" model mischaracterizes those in the middle as moderate or centrist, when in fact they are not interested in politics or policy at all and respond to political appeals perhaps on election day but not otherwise. It is easy to speak in the name of the "broad middle," as advocates of civility often do, but much harder to *lead* the broad middle, since it isn't necessarily looking for leadership and won't follow.

Places of public civility [in the United States] have something in common: They are places of political decision, the true loci of political and juridical resolution of disagreement.

The campaign trail, meanwhile, is strewn with an immense pile of abandoned pledges not to engage in "negative campaigning." For most politicians, civility is something to practice only until it puts you in danger of losing—which is a little short of a case for civility in politics.

It's also somewhere around here that we run into the phenomenon of advocates of civility denouncing the incivility of American politics in the most uncivil terms. It's possible that they don't realize the inconsistency of their position. More likely, they are merely engaged in a bit of political posturing intended to flatter themselves.

Models of Decorum

But there is a class of political speech where civility has indeed prevailed and continues to do so. A few examples: Arguments before the Supreme Court are models of civility. Although some of the justices are capable of wit and even sarcasm, and although those arguing before the Court tend to feel afterward that they really know what it means to be grilled, the atmosphere in the Court is circumspect and dignified.

Similarly, polling places on election day are models of decorum. In almost all cases, a hush prevails at the polling station. Advocates for opposing candidates are absent. The election workers maintain a scrupulous neutrality and a sober demeanor. In a presidential election involving 150 million voters in 2008, the number of accusations of voter intimidation at the polls was in the single digits.

Likewise, even strong disagreement on the floor of the Senate over a piece of legislation is noteworthy for its comity. The senators may not really mean it when they refer to each other as "my distinguished colleague," but the effect is real. The House floor is somewhat more raucous, but mainly during "Special Orders," a period after adjournment for the day when members can take the floor and speak on anything they wish. The "You lie!" episode was noteworthy for how unusual it was. Wilson faced criticism not only from Democrats but also from some Republicans, and he apologized for the incident. And it's worth noting that Wilson hurled his insult not as the House was performing its legislative function, but at a ceremonial occasion. During even the most contentious floor debates over legislation, members feel obliged to refrain from insulting each other personally, and when the question is called and members start voting, quietude prevails, at least until one side has crossed the threshold of victory.

The Loci of Political Decisionmaking

These three exemplary places of public civility have something in common: They are places of political decision, the true loci of political and juridical resolution of disagreement in this country. From the floor of Congress springs the law of the land. At polling places, the people render their judgment on who will represent them. In courtrooms, disinterested judges and juries make decisions affecting the liberty and property and sometimes the survival of the individuals appearing there. There are more such places, of course. Cabinet meetings at which questions of war and peace are on the table tend, by accounts, to be decorous if not solemn. Changes of command in the military are formal and ceremonial. Executive-branch agencies often conduct hearings into proposed new regulations, and the behavior of the parties appearing at them tends to be similarly decorous. State and local jurisdictions replicate federal institutions and practices and the decorum that goes with them.

Even though liberal societies do little or nothing to try to suppress incivility in the public square more generally, they are right ... to keep violent rhetoric and even uncivil rhetoric far from their places of decision-making.

One might say that people interacting on the floor of Congress, at the polls, or in a court of law act *as if* they and others were armed. There are, of course, *legal* sanctions for misbehavior in these places. Electioneering is illegal within a hundred yards of the polls. Judges have the power to order unruly persons removed from their courtrooms or jailed for contempt. Breach of the rules of the House and Senate is not criminal, but the sanction is more than merely social: It's constitutional. In an extreme case, these bodies have the authority to expel a member.

Keeping Violent Rhetoric Far from Decision-Making

But whence comes the importance of maintaining decorum in these places? Why constitutional and legal sanctions for misbehavior including incivility *here* but not elsewhere? Perhaps it's because incivility, including violent rhetoric (though such rhetoric is enabled by a liberal politics that has taken violence off the table), is nevertheless a reminder that politics is not everywhere, or necessarily permanently, free of violence. Violent rhetoric and its underlying sentiments, when coupled with the moment of actual political decision-making, can have disastrous consequences. It is therefore important to keep such rhetoric at some remove from the places and circumstances of political and juridical decision-making.

> *The danger of incivility to liberal political order has to be weighed against the danger posed by those who would recriminalize aspects of uncivil discourse through restrictions.*

One strain of criticism of classically liberal politics, and not an attractive one, regards its peaceable resolution of disagreements by means of elections, legislation, and juridical processes as an abeyance—a suspension, at best, of the essentially life-and-death quality of politics as such. This view sells the durability of liberal politics short. But even though liberal societies do little or nothing to try to suppress incivility in the public square more generally, they are right to remain wary of the return of violence to political disputation and to keep violent rhetoric and even uncivil rhetoric far from their places of decision-making.

Our liberal political order thus enables nonviolent incivility. The United States has been, perhaps, from its inception, a country more unruly than most other liberal polities. Our politics has always had an element of incivility to it. Not only do we have the liberal right to speak freely; we're also free from the authority of venerable traditional institutions such as a crown, an established church, a hereditary aristocracy, or an upper class expecting deference. It seems likely that a vestigial regard for or even fear of these sources of authority, which once *commanded* deference, may to a degree dampen incivility in the now-liberal polities where they retain influence.

Further, Americans have never had much cause to doubt their own free judgment—the judgment of their partisan opponents, certainly, but not themselves in general and collectively. Even slavery, the biggest stain on the American experience, predates the Founding and thus avoids a specifically American imprimatur; in addition, slavery was regional, and the blame for it therefore localized, rightly or wrongly. Nor did the liberalism of the American political order spring full blown from the 1789 Constitution. It developed over time. All things considered, there is nothing in the American experience remotely comparable to the Nazi period in the current German experience: occasion for bowel-shaking doubt and remorse on a national scale. Skepticism about what one might do with one's freedom, what freedom is capable of when it flourishes unconstrained by liberal order, could also have a dampening effect on the propensity for incivility.

Proliferating Platforms for Public Speech

Although incivility in America was present at the creation, it is nevertheless hard to deny that incivility in America has increased as platforms for public speech have proliferated. Everybody has a printing press and a microphone these days. Back when three commercial networks and a much smaller public broadcasting service ruled the television spectrum, when a few major newspapers enforced standards for newsworthiness of their own devising, when newspaper op-ed pages and a relatively small number of weekly or monthly or quarterly periodicals were the totality of outlets for the written expression of opinion—well, in those days, the norms governing civility in politics were easy to enforce. A de facto near-banishment from public speech was the available sanction for nonconformity to social norms, including public decorum. It worked both ways, however. As the 1960s activist Abbie Hoffman remarked in his autobiography, if he didn't feel like appearing on television on a particular day, he would write "F—K" on his forehead. Never failed.

Those days are over, never to return. And good riddance. If the price of civility was the return of gatekeeping on the scale of that bygone era in our media culture, it would be too high. It also seems to me that the danger of incivility to liberal political order has to be weighed against the danger posed by those who would recriminalize aspects of uncivil discourse through restrictions on "hate speech" and the like. The test for the unlawfulness of speech in a free society should remain violent content: a threat or incitement.

> *The breakdown of civility is not . . . the crisis in liberal political order some have made it out to be.*

Finally, there is the question of how damaging incivility in political discourse actually is. I raise this question as someone committed to civility; I have never called anyone a "douchebag," and I do not intend to start in with "asshat" now. My preferences aside, what is the empirical evidence?

The article by Brooks and Geer I cited at the beginning reports on the results of an elaborate experiment to measure people's comparative responses to positive political messages, negative messages (in the sense of negative campaigning), and uncivil negative messages (including those with ad hominem personal attacks included). People tend to discredit the value of messages that include personal attacks. But "upon close examination . . . we see no evidence that even the most despised of candidate messages—negative, uncivil, trait-based messages—are harmful to the democratic engagement of the polity." They continue:

> We see some suggestive evidence that those least-liked, least-valued kinds of messages may modestly stimulate two things that we tend to care a great deal about improving as a society: political interest and likelihood to vote. . . . Disagreements abound. Our data, however, suggest that the public will not melt in response to harsh exchanges—even those that are uncivil—and might even modestly profit from them in some cases.

It's certainly not the last word on the subject of the potential danger of incivility. But voter turnout, at least, has continued to increase since the article by Brooks and Geer appeared in 2007. If some people are turned off by the vitriol to the point of disengaging from participation in politics in the most basic way, by not voting, their numbers appear to be more than offset by other people tuning in.

The breakdown of civility is not, therefore, the crisis in liberal political order some have made it out to be—at least not yet. Decorum has not broken down where it counts most, at the places and times we are actually making our political decisions. We have a firebreak—partly Constitutional, partly statutory, partly customary—between incendiary political rhetoric and the political and juridical resolution of our disagreements.

If the inflammatory rhetoric managed to jump that firebreak, then we would have a serious problem. What we have now instead is freedom, incivility and all.

5

Liberals and Civility

Thomas Frank

Thomas Frank is a political analyst, historian, and columnist, who explores the rhetoric and impact of the culture wars in American political life and the relationship between politics and culture in the United States.

Worrying about incivility rather than vigorously countering crude conservative arguments about important issues weakens Democratic influence. Dodging the powerful rhetoric needed to address important economic and social issues does not reflect the once held image of a ready-to-do-battle Democratic Party. Rather than trying to be civil by discussing ancillary issues, Democrats should strongly counter conservative dogma that government involvement threatens liberty. Moreover, liberal leadership should directly address the laws made under conservative rule that created these economic and social challenges. If liberals want to achieve their goals, they must be willing to accept some incivility.

Now that their summer of bluster is over, conservatives may congratulate themselves on a job well done. The stout-hearted defenders of freedom declared that government could never work, sometimes citing examples of misgovernment drawn from periods of conservative rule to make their case.

They deplored the prospect of government intrusion into the economy, ignoring the fact that our current troubles are the consequence of government's withdrawal from the economy. They insisted that every government action, due to some mysterious law of freedom physics, produces an equal and opposite diminution of personal liberty.

Although these accusations were often crudely posed, conservatives deserve credit for showing up to the debate. The same cannot be said of the Democrats.

Why not simply beat the other side instead of complaining tearfully that they play too rough?

In truth, there has been no better time for a vindication of activist, Rooseveltian government since the 1930s. The laissez-faire faith lies in pieces around us. Conservative dogmatism lay behind many of the Bush administration's worst blunders, including some of the monumental screw-ups to which conservative pundits point when denouncing government generally.

But that is not how the Democrats have chosen to respond. Instead, they pine for civility, pretending that the argument comes down to the scary rhetoric issuing from the right. "I have concerns about some of the language that is being used, because I saw this myself in the late '70s in San Francisco," said House Speaker Nancy Pelosi last week. "This kind of rhetoric was very frightening, and it created a climate in which violence took place."

I have concerns about the rhetoric being used as well, and about the louts and the bullies who use it. But it seems clear that Mrs. Pelosi's aim is to avoid debate when she ought to be wading into the thick of it. Her team has the arguments; it has the facts; it has gale-force historical winds at its back: Why not give back as good as you get? Why not simply beat the other side instead of complaining tearfully that they play too rough?

Besides, retreating into some imagined genteel tradition offers little safety. For one thing, it goes against the old rough-and-tumble image of the Democratic Party and confirms instead the effete latte-and-sushi stereotype of recent years. For another, thanks to the 1960s and the Clinton presidency, morality and civility are concepts the right believes it owns. Republican legislators can heckle the president during a speech to a joint session of Congress and this will not change. No contradiction is stark enough to budge conservatives from the point: In fact, during the nation's last civility panic, even Ann Coulter was able to get in on the deploring.

President Obama, talking about his own civility concerns in an interview with CBS's Bob Schieffer on Sunday, said he understands that the health-care debate is a "proxy for a broader set of issues about how much government should be involved in our economy." What's strange is that he apparently doesn't believe he needs to take a side on those broader issues. Instead, he used his many interviews on Sunday to dodge those issues altogether, to insist that he isn't really proposing a grand scheme of government involvement at all, that those who worry about such things needn't be concerned.

Mr. Obama is probably the greatest orator my generation has produced; he swept into office last year with more of a mandate than any president since Ronald Reagan. Mrs. Pelosi commands a large majority in the House of Representatives. Both are talented politicians at the zenith of their careers. Facts and stories that make the liberal case are conveniently at hand—in every paper's headlines, in every voter's personal experiences.

Their opponents, meanwhile, have responded to the economic crisis by doubling down on the bad ideas that got us here in the first place. Their most prominent representative is the conspiracy-minded TV weeper Glenn Beck.

The health-care showdown should have been a one-sided blowout. And yet it is the Democrats who are running to the playground monitor and watching their support drain away.

Why? Because from the beginning they have understood the problem primarily as a technical consumer issue, not a bid for social justice in a manifestly unjust time. In their criticism of the insurance industry they have largely avoided terms like "profiteering" in favor of dry talk about lower costs and more competition—hardly an ideal platform from which to launch a crusade.

Conservatives, on the other hand, have been crusading nonstop since the days of Barry Goldwater. Every economic issue is a grand moral issue for them—this particular one, even in its lukewarm Senate Finance Committee version, is "a stunning assault on liberty," according to Sen. Jon Kyl (R., Ariz.)—and until liberals are prepared to contest those terms, they will have to live with a little incivility.

6

Incivility Has Lasting Psychological Consequences

Rebecca A. Clay

Rebecca A. Clay writes for the American Psychological Association, a research and professional organization of psychologists whose membership includes scientists, educators, clinicians, and consultants.

Not only does rude and uncivil behavior make life unpleasant, incivility influences behavior, concentration, and work performance. For example, studies show that those who frequent rant websites are more likely to express anger inappropriately. In addition, after reading rants, people's moods often worsen. Studies also show that listening to one-sided cell phone conversations creates more irritation than overhearing a two-sided conversation, as it is more difficult to ignore a one-sided conversation. Moreover, studies show these one-sided conversations reduce the ability to concentrate. Incivility in the workplace leads to lost productivity and in turn negatively impacts the bottom line. Fortunately, some efforts to reduce incivility in the workplace have proven successful.

Having worked as a bank teller for three and a half years before graduating from college in 2007, Michael T. Sliter, PhD, made a startling discovery: He found it easier to deal with the rare aggressive customers—people who shouted and spat—than people guilty of more subtle rudeness, such as not saying "please" or "thank you," questioning his competence or talking on a cellphone instead of focusing on the business at hand.

"With people who are overly aggressive—shouting, yelling, occasionally spitting on you—you can attribute that behavior to their personality," says Sliter, now an assistant professor of psychology at Indiana University-Purdue University Indianapolis. "At the end of the day, the type of customer who bothered me the most was just rude."

Sliter didn't let the experience get him down. Instead, he went on to become one of a growing number of psychologists conducting research on incivility. With polls suggesting most Americans feel civility is in decline, psychologists and other researchers are finding that rudeness does more than just make life unpleasant. It also has an impact on our ability to concentrate, our well-being and the bottom line.

Sparring with strangers on [rant] sites, the comments sections of mainstream news sites or even Facebook and Twitter isn't good for your mental health.

Technology's Role

A 2012 poll of 1,000 American adults by Weber Shandwick and Powell Tate in partnership with KRC Research found that about two-thirds of participants believed that incivility is a major problem. Almost three-quarters thought that civility has declined in recent years. While just 17 percent of participants reported being untouched by incivility, fewer reported personal experiences with incivility in certain contexts—on the road, while shopping, at work and in the neighborhood—than in last year's survey.

The poll did find a major increase in one area: online incivility and cyberbullying. Incidents doubled between 2011 and 2012, going from 9 percent of participants reporting that they had experienced such behavior to 18 percent.

Anonymity may be driving that phenomenon, says Ryan C. Martin, PhD, who chairs the University of Wisconsin-Green Bay psychology department. "When you're posting anonymously, you're more willing to say things you otherwise wouldn't say," says Martin. Plus, he says, the fact that you can respond immediately reduces impulse control.

So-called rant sites like JustRage.com encourage such behavior. But sparring with strangers on these sites, the comments sections of mainstream news sites or even Facebook and Twitter isn't good for your mental health, Martin and colleagues found in research published this year [2013] in *Cyberpsychology, Behavior and Social Networking*.

In one study, a survey revealed that people who frequent rant sites score higher on anger measures, express their anger more maladaptively and experience such negative consequences as verbal and physical fights more frequently than others. A second study, with college students as subjects, found that reading and writing such tirades typically worsened their moods.

Although both studies were small, says Martin, the findings debunk the conventional wisdom that venting is good for you and affirm other, larger studies, such as a 2002 study in the *Personality and Social Psychology Bulletin* by psychologist Brad J. Bushman, PhD, of The Ohio State University, who found the same thing.

Overhearing a cellphone conversation is much more annoying and distracting than hearing two people talking.

"I used to have a soccer coach who said, 'Practice makes permanent,'" he says. "That's what's happening here: If you get in the habit of venting anger in this way, it becomes your go-to mechanism for dealing with anger in all circumstances."

The cycle is also self-perpetuating, says Martin, adding that all of the online ranters in the first study reported that they felt calm and relaxed after ranting. "It's a rewarding experience for them from a conditioning perspective," he says. "But the long-term consequences of using that anger style are unhealthy."

The Cellphone Bubble

Cellphones are another target for incivility researchers. While most users no longer feel the need to shout into their phones, they may be so wrapped up "in their own little bubbles" that they don't realize they're blocking a sidewalk or holding up a line, says psychologist Veronica V. Galván, PhD, an assistant professor of psychological sciences at the University of San Diego.

But even more important is the fact that the very nature of cellphones, which allow others to hear only one side of the conversation, makes them uniquely irritating, she says. In a 2013 study published in *PLOS ONE*, Galván and colleagues found that overhearing a cellphone conversation is much more annoying and distracting than hearing two people talking. In the study, the researchers asked college students to do a concentration exercise while a confederate talked on a cellphone or when two people held the same conversation nearby. The students forced to overhear the one-sided conversation found themselves more irritated and distracted and were much more likely to remember the content of the conversation.

It's the missing half of the conversation that hijacks attention, says Galván. "In a cellphone conversation, part of the context is missing," she explains. "Every bit of information is a surprise since there's no context, and that seems to grab people's attention."

Other research, such as a 2010 study by Elizabeth L. Hay, PhD, and Manfred Diehl, PhD, of Colorado State University, in *Psychology and Aging*, has found that lack of perceived control over a stressor—such as being unable to escape an overheard cellphone conversation because you're on public transportation—can even lead to a physiological stress response, Galván adds.

Incivility from customers had a bigger impact on wellbeing than that from fellow employees.

Incivility in the Workplace

Incivility is also increasing at work, according to research by business professors Christine Porath, PhD, of Georgetown University, and Christine Pearson, PhD, of the Thunderbird School of Global Management. In a 2011 survey of workers, they found that half reported being treated rudely at least once a week—up from just a quarter in 1998.

All that rudeness comes at a price, warns Michael Sliter, the former bank teller. In a study of 120 bank tellers published last year in the *Journal of Organizational Behavior*, Sliter and his co-authors found that incivility—defined as low-intensity deviant behavior with ambiguous intent to harm the target in violation of workplace norms for mutual respect—made a big difference. Incivility from customers and co-workers increased tellers' absenteeism. It also decreased their sales performance, a rating that reflects the average number of recommendations to customers to open new accounts, try online banking, schedule a meeting about a mortgage or similar referrals that customers pursue.

In an earlier study of call center employees, published in the *Journal of Occupational Health Psychology* in 2011, Sliter and colleagues found that both the source and the target of incivility make a difference in outcomes. Incivility from customers had a bigger impact on well-being than that from fellow employees. And workers who are easy to anger seem to experience more negative effects from conflict with customers.

"Workplace incivility—people being rude or not refilling the coffee pot when it's empty—may seem like a relatively minor thing," says Sliter. "But the fact is that it's incredibly frequent and can have huge negative impacts on individuals."

Reducing Rudeness

Fortunately, as other research shows, it's possible to reduce workplace rudeness. Take the work of Michael P. Leiter, PhD, a psychology professor at Acadia University in Nova Scotia. Leiter has used an intervention called Civility, Respect and Engagement in the Workplace (CREW)—developed by a Veterans Health Administration team including psychologists Sue Dyrenforth, PhD, and Katerine Osatuke, PhD—to improve both civility and functioning in Canadian hospitals. The six-month intervention consists of units identifying specific concerns in workplace relationships, developing plans of action and evaluating their effectiveness.

Hospitals are fast-paced, multidisciplinary environments that depend on the smooth exchange of information, says Leiter. "If you offer a suggestion to someone who's then snarky at you, you'll hesitate before offering a suggestion to that jerk again," he says. "That interrupts the flow of information—and the stakes are high."

In a study of nearly 2,000 health-care providers in Canada published in the *Journal of Occupational Health Psychology* last year [2012], Leiter and his co-authors found that the CREW intervention led to improvements in civility, reductions in the amount of incivility people experienced from their supervisors and decreased distress, with improvements continuing even a year after the intervention ended. Attitudes such as job satisfaction and organizational commitment also saw sustained gains, although they didn't continue to improve afterward.

The changes hospital units made were easy, too. Emergency room staff, for example, agreed to tap a CREW pin on their lapels if they felt offended as a way of signaling that they needed to talk things out when they got a chance. Other units posted weather reports of the "emotional climate," with rainy days signaling rude behavior and prompting conversation.

"A big part of the intervention is just to get people to talk about their relationships rather than just getting ticked off with people and complaining to their friends," says Leiter. "That's part of your professional responsibility: to maintain good working relationships just like you maintain equipment and report breakdowns."

Leiter and his colleagues are now working with other health-care organizations and government agencies to spread the technique.

"Incivility is a solvable problem, not something you have to put up with," he says. "You don't have to wait until people get cynical or quit in disgust; it's something management can do something about."

7

Online Anonymity Increases Incivility

Richard Bird

Richard Bird is a freelance writer and world traveler with a special interest in the loss of civility in society. He writes on the topic of civility in his Collapse of Civility *blog.*

The ability to communicate anonymously in online communities poses a serious threat to civility. While innovation in communication technology has many benefits, some find ways to abuse these advances. Anonymous virtual personalities are free to spew their hate-filled venom online since they need not reveal their identity. In truth, these anonymous writers could be neighbors, relatives, or even community leaders, and most would not likely make these same comments in a public setting. Indeed, Internet anonymity creates a situation that encourages incivility since some people believe that they are no longer responsible for their behavior when they are invisible.

The availability of information, in both volume and speed, has been one of the key contributions made by technological innovation in fostering incivility. Familiarity, as the old saying goes, does breed contempt.

But, the greater threat to civility and civil behaviors is most certainly the cloak and veil that technology now provides to each and every one of us in our dealings with each other.

Embracing the Best and Worst

It is a fascinating condition of the human race; that we embrace both the best and worst that a technology has to offer. While I will spend some time today writing about chat rooms, avatars and hate-speech camoflauged as political commentary—the tendency for humans to use and misuse an innovation applies to stone wheels just as much as it does to bits and bytes.

The lowly hammer; it is most commonly used to build things. Hammering nails and framing houses, or fixing the dog house are natural activities for this technological innovation that took us beyond pounding some form of a peg with a large rock. But, that same hammer on many occasions, has been wielded and brandished as a weapon. Pounding a nail or bashing a skull—humans seem to find the light and dark within every single implement. Guns, axes, dynamite, atom smashing, oxycontin; the list of innovations that we corrupt is as long as history itself.

Computer based technology is no different, but the consequences for civility are just as concerning. The darkest aspect of technology, even darker than our continuous exposure to on-line fraud and theft, is the lack of responsibility and accountability that the anonymity of a virtual personality provides. The disconnectedness of being constantly connected manifests in the tendency for human beings to say things in an internet chatroom or on a comment string associated with a news story that they would never, ever say in the presence of a real live human being.

The Frightening Veil of Anonymity

I'll use an example to highlight how frightening the veil of anonymity has become, and how easy it is to be uncivil in the virtual world. I could link this posting to hundreds, if not thousands, of comments to news stories. But, a recent story in my hometown is certainly as good as any to drive home the point. On September 23, 2009, the *Columbus Dispatch* reported on a local speech given by Secretary of Transportation Ray LaHood. Mr. LaHood took issue with conservative talk show hosts, suggesting that their analysis and rhetoric ("trash talk") had contributed to a decline in civility.

As I have written before, I don't find that I learn much about civility by observing or researching politicians or political analysts. We live in an age where conservatives use inflammatory words and phrases but deny that they have any responsiblity for the potential consequences should things get out of control. And, in this same age, liberals are screaming for a more civil discourse and the complete elimination from memory of any of the bad behaviors and vitriolic rhetoric that they leveraged when they were in the minority.

> *The anonymity of the internet has created an environment where the absolute worst aspects of our human nature manifest themselves.*

I'm reminded of what Will Rogers [actor and witty author] had to say about the state of political behavior in the United States some 80 years ago—"I bet after seeing us, George Washington would sue us for calling him 'father.'". . .

Rather than addressing whether Mr. LaHood's argument is defensible (are conservative talk show hosts contributing to a decline in civility), the comments immediately focus on demanding that the reader subscribe to one political ideology or another. Since I am in the mood for quotes today, the seething anger and vicious statements made by commentators on this news story recalls a point by Oscar Wilde [Irish poet and playwright] "Democracy means simply the bludgeoning of the people by the people for the people."

Emboldened by Anonymity

Hate, racism, rants, venom—all of these uncivil aspects of discourse, and more, manifest themselves in the comments to this news story. Many of the people on this comment thread could be your neighbors, friends, aunts, uncles, parents, grandparents, your boss or your community leaders. Unfortunately, we can't tell, because no one knows for sure who they are really are. In fact, one of them might be you. With names like "the Truth," "Troll," "Legal American" and "Master Yoda" not only are we denied the opportunity to know who is writing, the writer is given carte blanche to be as uncivil as they want to be. Read some of the most antagonistic postings in this thread, and then wonder on whether the person who wrote it would be inclined to say the same thing—verbatim—in church or at a PTA meeting. Would they be so bold to stand up in a meeting of Rotarians, a Chamber of Commerce or a school board meeting and share the same sentiments? Not only is the answer a resounding "no," most of these writers would be personally embarassed to make such offensive comments in any public setting.

But, the internet changes everything. The upstanding citizen within our community that deems the anonymous "tagging" of a train box car with graffiti that points out any number of social ills in our inner city as a blight on society, sees no parallel to their own anonymous "tagging" of news stories and blog posts in the same light. The graffiti artist is a social misfit (as opposed to an artist), but an anonymous commentator spouting a hate filled response is not? The anonymity of the internet has created an environment where the absolute worst aspects of our human nature manifest themselves; stalking pedophilia, bullying to the point of driving someone to suicide, revenge postings of nude photographs of former girlfriends, boyfriends and spouses.

If you were invisible, and could not be held responsible for what you say or do—what would you do with such power? Maybe you don't need to think about an answer to this thought experiment. Maybe all you need to do is re-read some of the postings you have made in the vast anonymity of the internet. Maybe being invisible has made us much less civil.

8

Partisan Politics
Promotes Incivility

Michael Wolf

Michael Wolf is an associate professor of political science at Indiana University-Purdue University Fort Wayne.

Long before the tragic January 8, 2011, Tucson, Arizona, shooting that left six people dead and injured US representative Gabrielle Giffords, political incivility was growing. Although most agree that politics is rarely civil, currently political parties share little common ground and few Americans seek compromise, which often leads to incivility. In fact, surveys show that despite concerns about growing incivility, Americans from both parties want politicians to stand firm on the issues. In truth, some scholars argue that incivility in partisan politics is a sign of increased public engagement. Nevertheless, some claim that people should discuss political issues among their peers rather than obtain information from news sources partial to one party. Personal relationships may have a level of empathy that encourages greater civility.

Whether or not one believes that the Arizona shootings[1] were at all related to our current political environment,

1. On January 8, 2011, US representative Gabrielle Giffords and eighteen others were shot during a constituent meeting held in a supermarket parking lot in Tucson, Arizona. Six people died, including federal District Court Chief Judge John Roll; Gabe Zimmerman, one of Giffords's staffers; and a nine-year-old girl, Christina-Taylor Green. The shooter, Jared Lee Loughner, pled guilty to nineteen charges of murder and attempted murder.

Michael Wolf, "Disgusted by Discourse Public Concern with Incivility Rising, IPFM Research Finds," *Journal Gazette* [Ft. Wayne, IN], January 16, 2011. Copyright © 2011 by Michael Wolf. All rights reserved. Reproduced by permission.

the tragic events in Tucson have led to a widespread reflection on civility, or the lack of it, in our political discourse. Noting a rising incivility in political discussions in 2009, and with support from the IPFW [Indiana University-Purde University Fort Wayne] Department of Political Science and Office of Academic Affairs, the Center for Political Participation at Allegheny College began tracking public perceptions of incivility in politics in 2010. Our findings suggest that the public has become increasingly concerned about incivility.

Affiliates of both major parties simply blame the other side for incivility, while independents point at both parties.

A Civility Survey

With temperatures running high politically, the center fielded its first civility survey immediately after the vote on health care reform in March 2010. At that time, 48 percent of the public believed politics had become less civil since President [Barack] Obama took office.

We assumed the heated discourse that vote generated would be the high water mark of incivility, but we wanted to gauge how the campaign would affect these perceptions. We were stunned to find that things got worse by our September survey, with 58 percent of the public saying politics were less civil. In the days right before the November election, 63 percent of registered voters noted lower political civility.

Clearly the public noted mounting incivility well before Tucson. Some have blamed the tea party. Since most tea party identifiers in our surveys were also Republicans, we find no significant difference on their views. Much of the reason for incivility comes from the considerable chasm between Democrats and Republicans, and this makes it difficult to turn down the volume of debate.

A Partisan Chasm

The public agrees that politics are not civil, but there is not much common ground between the two parties on much else. In particular, Americans have different tastes in their news sources, hold their political opponents responsible for political incivility, and frequently have no appetite for political compromise.

Our findings confirm partisans gravitate toward different news sources. Democrats are more likely to read papers and Republicans are more apt to get news from radio. While all groups are most likely to get their news from television or the Internet, those are the very sources that can be the most partial to one party.

The problem is greater than partisan bias and demonizing opponents. Different news sources set different political agendas, so partisan opponents most likely do not even agree on what the biggest political problems are.

It is understandable why voters who want principled stands from politicians can stomach aggressive campaign fights, but at the same time, this is not conducive to civility.

Results from our question on who is responsible for incivility suggest a second obstacle to civility. Affiliates of both major parties simply blame the other side for incivility, while independents point at both parties. Very few partisans reflect on their own side's role in incivility. Why would they when, apparently, it's the other side's fault?

Registered voters' attitudes on compromise challenge civility even more fundamentally. When voters were asked which was more important in a politician, the ability to compromise to get things done, or a willingness to stand firm in support of principles, 51 percent wanted politicians to stand firm. Though there were strong differences between parties. Compromise was preferred by 74 percent of Democrats, whereas 73 percent of Republicans preferred politicians to stand firm. Granted, a politician can be civil and principled, but an easier route to civility comes from compromise.

Not wanting compromise has spillover effects on incivility. First, it increases the acceptance of campaign negativity. Forty-six percent of Americans said 2010 was the most negative campaign they had ever seen, with 87 percent of Democrats and 72 percent of Republicans saying the negative tone was bad for our democracy. Nevertheless, 55 percent of those Republicans who wanted politicians to stand firm also said the negative campaign tone made them more interested in participating, even though they said 2010 was the nastiest campaign ever and its tone was bad for our democracy. Preferring compromise, the campaign tone demobilized Democrats. It is understandable why voters who want principled stands from politicians can stomach aggressive campaign fights, but at the same time, this is not conducive to civility.

Unlike earlier times, each party's current ideological uniformity means the two parties stake out uncompromising positions on major issues.

Those results don't mean Republicans are uncompromising by nature. We do not have data for 2006, but that year Democrats were uncompromising with the [George W.] Bush administration and preferred politicians with principled stands against the Iraq war. When a party is in the minority, its members may be more likely to avoid compromise.

Regardless, new representatives and senators elected due to the vigor of principle-oriented Republicans can legitimately claim their mandate is *not* to compromise with Democrats. If the last Congress seemed uncivil, this new Congress has the potential to be even worse.

Partisan Polarization

Of all the reasons given for incivility, our survey finds that political parties are most frequently held as the main culprit. Like James Madison [fourth president of the United States], Americans have always distrusted parties for their propensity to divide.

So how did we end up with polarized parties? Historically, when confronting divisive issues, there was greater bipartisan ideological agreement. Since the civil rights era, however, southern conservative Democrats slowly shifted to the Republican Party, leaving few conservative Democrats. In the 1980s, northeastern liberals began turning away from Republicans, leaving few liberal Republicans. Unlike earlier times, each party's current ideological uniformity means the two parties stake out uncompromising positions on major issues. So there is little ideological crossover between the parties and little room for compromise.

This is not an indictment of strong partisan beliefs. In fact, scholars like Alan Abramowitz have noted that polarized partisan policy positions are an indication of greater political engagement and sophistication. Further, political observers have for years wished the public would care more about politics and participate more, so it is somewhat disingenuous to then want to undercut citizens' motivations. These motivations, however, may minimize civility.

The parties continue to purify themselves ideologically through primary elections. Moderates from both parties have struggled in primary elections in recent years against ideological challengers, leaving even fewer in Congress willing to compromise.

Increasing Civility

There are numerous suggestions long floated for increasing civility. Some call on cable news to seat less oppositional guests for debates. Others say those in Congress should pursue outside friendships with partisan opponents.

Indeed, despite their strong partisan differences, college political party leaders from 14 universities—including IPFW—posted 10 meaningful tips for improved civility on the center's website at a national conference in May 2010 at Allegheny College.

Differing political partisan views and disagreements are not the enemy of civility.

But citizens cannot control many of these methods for bringing back civility. Citizens can control their own comments. Rather than clamming up on divisive topics, citizens should discuss politics more one on one with friends, co-workers and neighbors of different political persuasions. We cannot decide media content or politicians' posturing, but we can control our deliberations. This is not Pollyannaish. Our findings showed the forces working against civility: different news sources, different sources of blame for incivility, and an aversion by many to politicians who compromise.

All of these can be short-circuited through discussion with those with different political views. Differing political partisan views and disagreements are not the enemy of civility. Meaningful one-on-one political disagreement is not the same as flaming opposing views on message boards or through blogs.

Scholars such as Robert Huckfeldt and Diana Mutz have found that disagreement in political discussion leads to more knowledge, greater understanding of the other side's rationale, and better deliberation about candidates—even among partisans.

Is it risky to pipe up with a counterpoint? Yes, and it may be uncomfortable. But is less political information superior to this discomfort? Is the continued gravitation toward permanent opposing camps better than mild disagreement?

What scholars actually find is relationships bring with them a level of empathy, which can lead people toward more tolerance and, as a result, more civility. Ironically, turning the volume up, even if just one-on-one political disagreement, can lead to greater civility.

9

Uncivil Political Bullies Threaten the Democratic Process

Michael Winship

Michael Winship is a senior writer at Public Affairs Television in New York City.

Although uncivil bullying is not new in politics, people should not tolerate, or worse, applaud this behavior. Indeed, people should censor political candidates that threaten those who question their claims or counter their point of view. For example, candidates whose security guards detain and handcuff journalists who ask questions about their policies deserve censure not support. Such uncivil behavior threatens the First Amendment right of Americans to speak freely, although some who employ these bullying techniques claim to be the US Constitution's greatest defenders. People should stand up to these bullies and call them to task. Failing to do so will only lead to more incivility and bullying in the public arena.

One of the most memorable moments in television coverage of American politics came during the Democratic National Convention in Chicago in 1968. Out on the streets, anti-Vietnam war demonstrations were attacked viciously by law enforcement officials in what later was described in an official report as "a police riot."

Inside the convention hall, tightly controlled by the political machine of the city's notorious Mayor Richard J. Daley, CBS correspondent Dan Rather was attempting to interview a delegate from Georgia who was being removed from the floor by men in suits without ID badges. One of them slugged Rather in the stomach, knocking him to the ground. As the reporter struggled to get his breath back, from the anchor booth, Walter Cronkite exclaimed, "I think we've got a bunch of thugs here, Dan!"

It was an uncharacteristic outburst from America's Most Respected Newsman, indicative of just how terrible the violence was both inside and out and how shocking it was for a journalist to be so blatantly attacked while on the air by operatives acting on behalf of politicians.

The Pulpit of Bullies

As appalling as that 1968 assault was, thuggery is nothing new in politics; it transcends time, ideology and party. But what's even more disturbing in 2010 is how much of the public, especially many of those who count themselves among the conservative adherents of the Tea Party, is willing to ignore bullying behavior—and even applaud it—as long as the candidate in question hews to their point of view.

Here in New York State, of course, we have Republican gubernatorial candidate Carl Paladino, who combines the boyish charm of J. Edgar Hoover with the sunny quirkiness of Pol Pot.[1] So extreme are Paladino's views, so volatile his temper, that even [media mogul] Rupert Murdoch's right wing *New York Post* has endorsed Democrat Andrew Cuomo, which is a

---

1. Pol Pot, a Cambodian revolutionary, led the Khmer Rouge, a revolutionary army, from 1963 until 1997. He became the leader of Cambodia on April 17, 1975. As dictator, he forced urban dwellers to relocate to the countryside to work in collective farms and forced labor projects. As a result of executions, forced labor, malnutrition, and poor medical care, 25 percent of the Cambodian population died—an estimated one to three million people.

bit like the Vatican newspaper *L'Osservatore Romano* dissing the Pope and singing the praises of Lutherans.

Doubtless this is in part because Crazy Carl, as he is affectionately known to many, almost came to blows with the *Post*'s state political editor, the redoubtable Fred Dicker, shouting "I'll take you out, buddy!" at Dicker after the journalist asked Paladino for evidence to back up allegations the candidate was making against Cuomo and Paladino claimed the paper was harassing his out-of-wedlock daughter.

The *Post* had to admit that Paladino is "long on anger and short on answers . . . undisciplined, unfocused and untrustworthy—that is, fundamentally unqualified for the office he seeks."

Support for Bullies

Okay, Paladino will lose, but in other parts of the country, Tea Party-supported candidates with a similar bullying, threatening attitude, or who seem to surround themselves with such people, are more likely to win. Republican Allen West, endorsed by Sarah Palin [former Alaska governor and Republican vice presidential cadidate in 2008] and John Boehner [Republican congressman and speaker of the US House of Representatives], is leading in his race against incumbent Democratic Representative Ron Klein in South Florida's 22nd Congressional District [West defeated Klein in the November 2010 election].

A retired Army lieutenant colonel, West resigned from the military, according to the progressive website ThinkProgress .org, "while facing a court martial over the brutal interrogation of an Iraqi man: according to his own testimony during a military hearing, West watched four of his men beat the suspect, and West said he personally threatened to kill the man. According to military prosecutors, West followed up on his threat by taking the man outside and firing a 9mm pistol near his head, in order to make the man believe he would be shot."

You can't make this stuff up: Last week [October 2010], NBC News reported that West has been communing with a notorious Florida motorcycle gang, the Outlaws, which the Justice Department alleges has criminal ties to arson, prostitution, drug running, murder and robbery. And on Monday, West could be heard at a rally urging some bikers—also with Outlaw connections—to "escort" out a Klein staffer who was video recording the event. "Threats can be heard on the videotape," said a reporter from NBC's Miami affiliate. "West supporters forced him to get back into his car."

Hooliganism and casual trampling of First Amendment rights from people who claim to embrace the Constitution as holy writ is symptomatic of a deeper problem.

The West campaign responded that "the latest attacks aimed at associating . . . Allen West with a criminal and racist gang are completely baseless and nothing short of a hatchet job." So what's with the photograph of him glad-handing bikers who according to NBC brag about their association with the Outlaws? And why did West tell a supporter to back off when concern was expressed about "criminal organization members in leather" appearing at West's campaign rallies?

Using Bullies to Silence Criticism

Which brings us to Joe Miller, the Republican and Tea Party candidate for the United States Senate from Alaska. On Sunday [October 2010], at a Miller town hall, private security guards hired by the campaign—two of whom were moonlighting, active duty military—took it upon themselves to detain a reporter pursuing Miller with questions, placed him under citizen's arrest and handcuffed him—then threatened to detain two other reporters who were taking pictures and asking what was going on.

The plainclothes rent-a-cops, complete with Secret Service-type earpieces and Men in Black-style neckties and business suits, come from an Anchorage-based outfit called DropZone Security, which also runs a bail bond service and an Army-Navy surplus store—with one of those anti-Obama "Joker" posters pasted to its window. One-stop shopping for the vigilante militiaman in your life—kind of like that joke about the combination veterinarian-taxidermist: either way you get your dog back.

All of this would be funnier if not for the fact that this kind of hooliganism and casual trampling of First Amendment rights from people who claim to embrace the Constitution as holy writ is symptomatic of a deeper problem.

The anger of the electorate is understandable: politicians and politics as usual have given voters much about which to be mad; furious, in fact. But bullying is different. It comes from insecurity and fear, and lashes out with tactics of intimidation. To dismiss it as merely a secondary concern and say "I'll take my chances" as long as the candidates in question agree with you is dangerous. Scuffling with the press and others may seem minor, but it's just the beginning. In states where there is early balloting, already there are allegations of voter harassment, primarily in minority neighborhoods.

The only way to fight back against bullies and thugs is to stand up and tell them to go to hell. To do otherwise is to give an inch and prepare to be taken for the proverbial mile. That way lies madness. And worse.

10

Imitation of Media Images Leads to Incivility

Joseph Cramer

Joseph Cramer, a practicing pediatrician for thirty years, is a fellow of the American Academy of Pediatrics and an adjunct professor of pediatrics at the University of Utah.

That society is becoming less civil should come as no surprise, as people mimic what they see every day. In truth, uncivil behavior has become an accepted part of movies and television today. Hollywood heroes solve problems in anger and with violence. Sadly, people imitate the very things they have created to reflect American culture. As long as moral training comes from images of antisocial, violent, and selfish behavior, people can expect growing incivility. Parents who do not limit the time their children watch television and movies or fail to ensure that their children see images of kindness and unselfishness, deserve the uncivil country they get.

There was recent earth-shattering news. Children behave according to what they see in the media.

Now to be a professional who has studied and cared for kids, I am restrained from shouting, "Duh!"

Why is anyone wondering why we are less civil in society? We see it acted out every day of our lives.

Goethe [German author and politician] said, "You see what you know," meaning we recognize our knowledge expressed in the world around us. I submit that we "know what we see." We know how to act unkind because we see it in interactions with others. We become angry more often because that is what the movie hero does. We think about being hurt or hurting others because that is how good guys take down the bad guys.

Imitating What We See

Solutions of complex, real problems come straight out of a Hollywood plot. We imitate our own imitations. If a bad man has a gun, a good man with a gun will shoot and kill him.

The human body learns by re-enacting what it sees. This is not due to the invention of Philo T. Farnsworth [the inventor of television]; it is how culture transmits rapidly between generations. If our ancestors saw someone throw a spear at a bear, then getting food would be that much easier for the children and their children.

Our systems of education, entertainment, politics, wealth segregation and moral training are producing exactly the results we get in our children and in our communities.

We tell our children every day to be a good example. Why? Because we want others to see and then act similarly. Treating someone as you want them to treat you is a codification of this seeing and knowing, seeing and doing.

With the advance of technology, we learn by acting as if in simulations. Fighter jets no longer have a two-seat version for pilot training. Earlier planes would have one seat for the cadet and the other for the experienced trainer. Now, it is all done with simulations. You know what you see.

The re-enactment of scenarios of in-flight emergencies are experienced repeatedly in order to train non-verbal memory to act more quickly, "without thinking." That is what watching anything does to us if we do it enough with the right sensory input. We stop thinking and just act out spontaneously.

An article in the March [2013] medical journal, *Pediatrics*, concludes that since no one follows the advice to limit screen time, then make sure children watch acts of kindness and self-lessness. While the idea of pro-social learning is not new, it is the sad realization that we as a country cannot turn off our insatiable appetite for action and adventure that disappoints.

Our brains from birth are built to suck in information. Children especially are programmed to learn emotions and relationships from their mothers at the instance of their birth. It is the many acts of sensitive reaction to stress that instruct the infant about relationships. "Falling in love for the first time" is an act of imitation. We reflect back to our mothers the love in their eyes and in their faces.

We can also fall out of love with what we see and feel as we grow. Trans-generational poverty is no aberration of one person or group, but a product of a nationwide classroom of knowing what we see. Heroes are not the scholars of Nobel or the authorship of Pulitzer. Instead, the community is the tutor. In some cases, the flashing police lights illuminate the stage and the crime-scene yellow tape keeps the viewing audience back.

We deserve the country we inhabit. "A system is perfectly designed to produce the exact results it gets," the theory says. Our systems of education, entertainment, politics, wealth segregation and moral training are producing exactly the results we get in our children and in our communities.

Unless we start watching with our children different programs, we are fated to do what we see. We imitate our imitations. As long as they are anti-social, violent or absent of empathy, we will see more articles where we will all start to say, "Duh."

11

Media Can Build Civility

Sarah van Gelder and Brooke Jarvis

Sarah van Gelder is executive editor and Brooke Jarvis is web editor for YES! magazine, a publication that reflects the views of YES!, a national, nonprofit media action organization.

Media need not endorse fear and hatred. In fact, news media can instead promote civil, productive debate and help opposing camps find common ground. The tragic January 8, 2011, shooting in Tucson, Arizona, that left six people dead and injured US representative Gabrielle Giffords, made clear that words do influence behavior. Although disagreement is human and part of the democratic process, repeating violent and hate-filled language that demonizes those with opposing views and plays on people's insecurities during challenging times is irresponsible. Thus, rather than simply repeating inflammatory claims from both sides of a controversial political issue, media should provide context, focusing on the root causes and getting people to ask questions that will lead to effective solutions.

"Just as media outlets have been used to create a pervasive sense of fear, they have also been used to convince people that conflict is inevitable. This leaves media consumers resigned to the notion that conflict will happen."

Those words could have been used to describe an increasingly hostile and provocative media in the United States. In fact, they were written to describe the use of the media to incite Hutus to slaughter their Tutsi neighbors in Rwanda, resulting in hundreds of thousands of deaths [in 1994].

The media can choose to provoke the least stable, most trigger-happy sectors of the population. Or it can strengthen democracy, civility, and the rule of law.

After [twenty-two-year-old gunman] Jared Loughner opened fire at a political event for Congresswoman Gabrielle Giffords in Tucson, Arizona[1] [on January 8, 2011], attention quickly focused on the role that divisive and aggressive media may have played in his actions. Pima Country Sheriff Clarence Dupnik lamented "the vitriol that comes out of certain mouths about tearing down the government."

Members of the media were quick to defend themselves. Any discussion of possible political motives, the editors of the *National Review* wrote, constitute a "vile attempt to tar the opposition with the crimes of a lunatic so as to render illegitimate the views of about half of America."

The reasons for Loughner's actions are still unclear, and evidence suggests that he is mentally ill. We can't know at this point what role media provocation may have played in his decision. Indeed, his actions raise as many questions about our policies on gun ownership and mental illness as they do about our political climate.

At the very least, though, this should be a moment to reflect on the role that media can play in directing the political dialogue in this country. It can, as we know, promote fear, hatred, and extremism. Can it also lead us to greater civility and more productive debate?

Violence and the Media

Sadly, the Arizona shooting is only the latest evidence that words do have consequences.

---

1. Loughner pled guilty to nineteen charges of murder and attempted murder in connection with the shooting that injured Giffords, his target, and killed six people, including federal judge John Roll and nine-year-old bystander Christina-Taylor Green.

On July 18 [2010], Byron Williams was approached by California state police for driving erratically on Interstate 580. A firefight [shootout] ensued—remarkably, all survived—and Williams later admitted he had been on his way to attack the ACLU [American Civil Liberties Union] and the non-profit Tides Foundation. Why Tides? According to Media Matters, Fox News commentator Glenn Beck had verbally attacked the Tides Foundation 29 times in the 18 months before the attempted shooting.

The media can choose to provoke the least stable, most trigger-happy sectors of the population. Or it can choose to strengthen democracy, civility, and the rule of law.

After then-vice presidential candidate Sarah Palin accused presidential candidate Barack Obama of "palling around with terrorists," the Secret Service reported a dramatic increase in threats against Obama.

There are many more stories of threats and vandalism directed at private citizens and public officials, and the links to the violent rhetoric from right-wing media personalities and politicians is chilling. One Texas man, who called the office of Senator Debbie Stabenow and threatened "We'll get you . . . like we did RFK [Robert F. Kennedy]; like we did MLK [Martin Luther King, Jr.]," told FBI [Federal Bureau of Investigation] officers he was worried the government would take Sean Hannity and Rush Limbaugh off the air as a result of the "Fairness Doctrine."

Another Way

The media can choose to provoke the least stable, most trigger-happy sectors of the population. Or it can choose to strengthen democracy, civility, and the rule of law. When the former Yugoslavia was erupting in ethnic cleansing and massacres, Macedonia's ethnically diverse population remained at peace. South Africa made the transition from Apartheid to majority rule largely without violence. In these and other places, media that highlighted the humanity of all involved played a role, according to the U.S.-based Search for Common Ground.

Whipping up fear and hatred, demonizing those with conflicting opinions, using violent language, playing on the insecurity and distrust that so easily arise during difficult times—these are irresponsible and wrong.

Instead of simply repeating the anger and allegations of each side—which may have the effect of deepening the conflict or inciting violence—journalists are in a unique position to uncover the causes of conflict and discover opportunities for finding common ground. The Conflict Resolution Network advises journalists to:

- Focus on the root causes of problems, not just positions or back-and-forth arguments.

- Ask questions that get people thinking about solutions and common ground: "What would be possible if this problem were fixed?" "What would it take to solve this problem?" "What is it that you *do* want?" "What would satisfy you?"

- Avoid simplistic divisions between good and bad. Don't encourage or sensationalize personal attacks.

- Report areas of agreement as well as disagreement.

- Think of emotions as symptoms that point to where the real problems are. What clashes of values, needs, or scarce resources are causing an emotional response?

Disagreement over policy is part of a healthy democracy, and conflict is human. But whipping up fear and hatred, demonizing those with conflicting opinions, using violent language, playing on the insecurity and distrust that so easily arise during difficult times—these are irresponsible and wrong. Especially when the media is capable of so much more.

12

Persuasion as the Cure
for Incivility

John I. Jenkins

John I. Jenkins is president of the University of Notre Dame and a member of the board of directors for the Commission on Presidential Debates.

Since public polls reveal that many Americans are frustrated by uncivil political campaigns that avoid discussion of the issues, candidates and commentators should consider the more civil approach—reasoned persuasion. Rather than demonizing and distorting the views of opponents, people should try to persuade others of the benefits of their position on an issue. Moreover, to answer objections, persuasion requires understanding the views of others, which in turn requires that people treat others with respect. Indeed, despite the celebration of bluntness and coarseness, incivility discourages reasoned debate while civility allows the views of others to be heard.

What If, Instead of
Demonizing Opponents, We Took
Steps to Persuade Them?

Several decades ago, my predecessor as the president of the University of Notre Dame, the Rev. Theodore M. Hesburgh, was presented with a dilemma. A Jewish student, after repeated hazing by some kids in his dorm, had left campus and gone home. After thinking it over, Father Hesburgh sum-

John I. Jenkins, "Persuasion as the Cure for Incivility; What If, Instead of Demonizing Opponents, WE Took Steps to Persuade Them?," *Wall Street Journal*, January 8, 2013. Reprinted with permission of Wall Street Journal. Copyright © 2013 Dow Jones & Company, Inc. All rights reserved worldwide.

moned the perpetrators. "Pack your bags," he told them. "Go find your friend. Either you persuade him to come back to Notre Dame, or you don't come back."

The approach worked for everyone concerned, and it may offer an idea for easing the incivility that marks much public discourse and leads to political stalemate. We need to try harder to persuade one another—to try to get people to change their minds.

There isn't nearly enough persuasion going on in America today, and there was too little, in the view of many citizens, in the past presidential campaign. A postelection Pew poll found that the 2012 campaign was a "frustrating experience" for many voters: 68% said there was more "negative campaigning and mudslinging," with less discussion of issues.

The recent fiscal-cliff negotiations might have ended in a budget deal, but the rhetoric during the wrangling was hardly of the persuasive variety.

That is likely because much of the election campaigning and much of the budget discussion wasn't designed to change anyone's mind, but instead to encourage people to believe more deeply what they already believed—not about policies, for the most part, but about the villainy of the other side.

What if, instead of dealing with opponents by demonizing them and distorting their views, we were to take some steps to persuade them?

In the presidential campaign, the negative ads and speeches may have been unfortunately effective. A *Washington Post-ABC News* poll from last summer reported that 70% of Republicans saw President Obama in a strongly unfavorable light, and 57% of Democrats had a very unfavorable view of Gov. Romney. These were historically very high numbers for two presidential contenders.

As a country, we seem to have become the factions James Madison warned against in 1787, when he wrote: "A zeal for different opinions concerning religion, concerning government, and many other points . . . have, in turn, divided mankind into parties, inflamed them with mutual animosity, and rendered them much more disposed to vex and oppress each other than to cooperate for their common good." A more earnest effort to persuade one another could help remedy many of the problems we face.

I confess that I am deeply biased. I am a university president with a strong belief in the power and importance of a liberal arts education. I believe that deep and candid dialogue, marked by many acts of courtesy and gestures of respect, is a discipline that brings us nearer the truth about ourselves, about our opponents, about human nature, and about the subject under debate. To shut down this source of wisdom because we are too angry to hear the other side is a tragic setback in our quest for knowledge and our hope for a healthy society.

What if, instead of dealing with opponents by demonizing them and distorting their views, we were to take some steps to persuade them? I don't mean to suggest that one could persuade a stalwart partisan to switch parties, but perhaps one could persuade another that a particular policy or a position is "not as bad as you think."

A more sincere effort to persuade one another would remind us why the Founders believed this country could improve on history.

If I am trying to persuade others, I first have to understand their position, which means I have to listen to them. I have to appeal to their values, which means I have to show them respect. I have to find the best arguments for my position, which means I have to think about my values in the context of their concerns. I have to answer their objections, which means I have to work honestly with their ideas. I have to ask them to listen to me, which means I can't insult them.

If we earnestly try to persuade, civility takes care of itself.

Civility is sometimes derided in the modern world, where bluntness and even coarseness have somehow come to be celebrated in many quarters. But civility is not a minor virtue. It is not an attempt to impose someone's notion of courtesy, and it is certainly not an attempt to suppress speech. Civility is what allows speech to be heard. It is an appeal to citizens never to express or incite hatred, which is more dangerous to the country than any external enemy.

A more sincere effort to persuade one another would remind us why the Founders believed this country could improve on history: We were the first society in many centuries with the chance to use free speech and sound argument to debate our way toward a better future.

That path is still open, and as promising as ever.

13

College Classrooms Can Be More Civil

P.M. Forni

P.M. Forni, author of Choosing Civility *and* The Civility Solution, *is a professor of Italian literature at Johns Hopkins University, where he directs the Civility Initiative.*

College students have become increasingly disrespectful and disengaged. Not only do students text and watch television on their portable devices during class but when unhappy with their grades, some send profane messages and even threats. Faculty can, however, establish civility in their classrooms by creating a formal learning environment and helping students see the value of learning. In addition, faculty can help students distinguish between what on the Internet is valuable and what is not. Moreover, in a world where students can easily retrieve information, faculty must explain the benefits of retention. Indeed, to relieve the tension in professor-student relationships, faculty must make clear that the knowledge they have to share is valuable and worth student respect.

The professing of knowledge used to rest on the firm foundation of the principle of authority. Most students granted their teachers respect and sometimes deference as a matter of course. That foundation has been crumbling for at least three generations. The new digital technology has virtually razed it.

P.M. Forni, "The Civil Classroom in the Age of the Net," *Thought & Action* [The NEA Higher Education Journal], Fall 2008, pp. 15–22. Copyright © 2008 by National Education Association. All rights reserved. Reproduced by permission.

As college teachers, it is imperative that we realize what this means for our relationship with our students and for the future of education.

Increasing Classroom Rudeness

In his *Chronicle of Higher Education* column, the pseudonymous Thomas H. Benton articulated a concern of many of today's faculty:

> Whatever the explanation, I sometimes feel stung by students' rudeness. I try to make my classes interesting and relevant, and I care about their learning. I try to conduct myself in a kindly but professional manner. But, more and more, I think the student culture of incivility is a larger impediment to their success than anything they might fail to learn about Western Civilization or whatever it is I am teaching.

For quite some time, we have observed that the disengaged, disrespectful, and unruly student behavior that used to be confined to secondary schools has reached higher education. In college classrooms across the U.S., tardiness, unfamiliarity with assigned readings, and unjustified absences are routine. So are chit-chatting, e-mailing, and instant-messaging. In large lecture halls where ringtones jar and jangle, students have been spotted reading newspapers and even watching television on their portable sets. Virtually no academic term goes by in which instructors don't open their inboxes to find e-mail that is inappropriately informal, unreasonably demanding, or both. After receiving less-than-stellar grades, legions of students cry foul. The arsenal of the disgruntled includes profanities, threats, and physical abuse. It may not be widely known, but college teachers are bullied too.

How did we get to this? Many students are simply not prepared to engage in serious academic work and do not know how they are expected to behave on campus. Most of them bring a consumer mentality to school and very little concern about approval from the older generation. That their own generation was raised on oversized portions of self-esteem is part of the problem, not to speak of their massive exposure to coarse popular culture on television and the Net. Of course, professors are not blameless either. We can be unfair, unhelpful, disillusioned, disengaged, arrogant, and sarcastic. And sometimes, just as our new breed of students is not prepared for college, we are not prepared for them.

As you foster . . . a learning environment where restraint, respect, and consideration are the norm, your students learn better and more.

The Net is a case in point. We know that it plays a major role in the shaping of the young, but how many of us have a strategy in place to cope with the challenge that this poses to education? In the last decade, first-year-experience programs have been sprouting up at many two-year and four-year colleges. When expertly managed, they have been invaluable assets, helping students learn how to behave civilly with both peers and teachers. However, these programs are not enough. If we want to slow down the continuing decline of traditional civil interaction on American college campuses, we must train ourselves too. In the following pages, I have collected a few reflections on the challenges we all face as college teachers and on ways of responding to them that have been working for me.

Establish a Climate of Relaxed Formality

Even in the radically informal times in which we live, I cannot be alone in believing that positive pedagogical results require a modicum of formality. It is, in part, through formality that you convey that there is value in what is taking place in class. Formality is the homage that intelligence pays to value. I concede that there may be circumstances in which asking your students to address you by your first name is the thing to do;

I just have not experienced them often. Your students are not your pals. Boundaries between roles should remain solid. Go for an Aristotelian happy medium between stilted formality— the kind that makes you aloof and discourages dialogue—and chumminess. Call it relaxed formality. I have addressed all my students as Mr., Miss, and Ms. throughout my teaching career and never had reason to regret it. If they seem to like it, in the second half of the semester I will switch occasionally to their first names. Students appreciate much more the informal address when we do not grant it outright, but rather as the result of a degree of familiarity they have achieved with us after hours of class-work.

I do not use juvenile jargon for effect, and only occasionally will I use an informal expression picked from the realm of popular culture if I see a pedagogical advantage in doing so. My private life remains so. Still, on occasion and with cause, I will disclose something personal—without indulging in idle chit-chat or gossip. I encourage my students frequently, often with a smile, but I am firm in expecting undivided attention for whoever has the floor, be it the instructor or a student. This style of interaction has helped me build a civil environment in which I and my students can be at our best as we teach and learn.

As you foster (through relaxed formality) a learning environment where restraint, respect, and consideration are the norm, your students learn better and more. In turn, their success in learning will have a positive effect on their classroom behavior. Non-disruptive behavior reinforces learning and vice-versa. This is the virtual circle you want to put in place in the everyday exercise of your profession. This is what defines a job well-done in the classroom.

Distinguishing the Trivial

The notion of value is woven together with that of difference. Recognizing and accepting difference is the premise of our recognizing and accepting value. Unfortunately, one major aspect of their experience with the Net inclines our students not to perceive difference. On the Net *every single thing* is equidistant from *every other thing* and from the person at the keyboard. It takes the same amount of time and the same effort to access *anything* you wish. The fact that one can as easily conjure up the Bible as *Mad* magazine erodes some of the difference between the two. When everything comes from the same source—the mysteriously endless and spaceless warehouses of the Net—everything reveals itself under a varnish of equivalence. To quote [American novelist] Philip Roth, "everything goes and nothing matters."

Anger (or even simple disaffection) can make students behave poorly—not only with their teachers, but with anyone else on campus as well.

I believe that part of my job as a teacher is to convey the notion that although the Net may conceal it, a hierarchy of values does exist and does matter. No matter what the topic of my class is, I often find myself using the material as a primer in moral philosophy. If we are reading poetry, we discuss the ethics of reading poetry: Why are we reading poetry? Can we justify this expenditure of time, money, and energy on moral grounds? How can we locate the value in what we are doing? Is there something more important that we should be doing instead? Go through the Net with your students, educating their critical eye. Open a conversation on what makes information trivial or important. Make discussing values a recurring exercise. When your students become more invested in the notion of value, they will find value in a class that questions its own value and behave more respectfully and considerately in class. Respect takes root in the presence of perceived value.

Sell Your Product and Yourself

Two current ways of looking at knowledge add disaffection and tension to the lives of teachers and students on today's campuses. They are: knowledge retention and knowledge retrieval. Many teachers and professors profess the former. For them knowledge is something to acquire and retain forever. Most students are partial to the latter. They look at knowledge as something to access when needed. For them, the Net is the repository of information of choice. The Net is where they go to have all their questions answered, be it the name of Alexander the Great's teacher, or how cathecolamines work. This devalues the figure of the teacher as a provider of knowledge. "I don't really need you, I have the Net," is the unspoken and sometimes subconscious belief that many students bring to the classroom; hence, there exists less incentive to pay attention in class, more boredom, more frustration, and more disruptive behavior.

My students and I have agreed upon codes of behavior— either oral or written—regulating our relationship during the term of classes.

Then, to make matters worse for them, that very professor whose image is so diminished in their eyes proceeds to evaluate them according to traditional standards. The professor expects retention of knowledge from students for whom retrieval on demand is the only way that makes sense. Not only are they unable to see the point of retaining, they do not know how to read to retain. Poor performance in tests follows. When students receive low grades, their disappointment and resentment are fueled by the perceived unfairness of it all: having paid good money for a bad grade, and for an education they see as obsolete. Anger can ensue. And, of course, anger (or even simple disaffection) can make students behave poorly—not only with their teachers, but with anyone else on campus as well.

Defending Retention

Be proactive. Bring forward the retention/retrieval divide, making sure you are well-prepared to defend the former without dismissing the latter. It goes without saying that retrieval according to necessity must become second nature in a world saturated with information. At the same time, make very clear that retention is crucial to our cognitive and emotional functioning. Our very ability to function in the world needs a solid structure of notions that we acquire and retain, be they historical, philosophical, literary, artistic, astronomical, musical, or other. Without reference to retained knowledge, there is no effective thinking. Without effective thinking, no wise choices are possible, and the good life is nothing but a chimeric abstraction. The outstanding leaders of tomorrow will be people with a rich inner structuring of possessed notions *and* a great ability to retrieve information.

Explain the benefits in taking the class, and taking the class from *you*. Go over what your role will be in a journey of cognitive and emotional growth that will take your students from information to knowledge and from knowledge to wisdom. This is easier to do in humanities classes, but science teachers will have to imagine new ways to get through to their students as well. Students need to understand what they can get from attending your class that they would not from sitting in their dorms in front of a digital screen. We need to present ourselves as necessary and authoritative mediators between the Net and our students, as the credible knowledge professionals who can teach them how to think about the information they retrieve. The alternative is to fade into obsolescence. Do not overpromise, however. Tell them what the class is not going to do for them. This is also the moment to touch upon the workload and discourage attendance by students who find it incompatible with their degree of motivation or availability of time and energy. I bring with me an at least subliminal awareness (if such a thing exists) of the new instructor-student dynamics brought about by the digital revolution every time I teach. It keeps me on my toes, making me want to convey content and meaning in ways that are insightful, challenging, and memorable.

Stipulate a Fair Covenant

If you have been dealing with a widespread student attitude mixing disengagement with disregard, you are not alone. Millions of educators around the world are in your same position. A tool of choice to make things better is to make your expectations explicit. For the past several years, my students and I have agreed upon codes of behavior—either oral or written—regulating our relationship during the term of classes. In the absence of compelling reasons not to do so, go for the written covenant.

At the top of a sheet of paper, under the heading "What I Expect from You," list entries such as:

"That you be punctual for every class."

"That you do not receive or make telephone calls."

"That you respect what I and your fellow students have to say."

"That you come to class ready to ask and answer questions of substance on the day's readings."

"That you be mindful of time constraints when making presentations."

"That you will concentrate exclusively on this course during class hours."

Use the bottom half for your own list of commitments, "What You Can Expect from Me":

"That I will be punctual for every class."

"That I will give everybody a fair share of my attention."

"That I will prepare you for your tests."

"That I will grade the quality of your work rather than the amount of time and effort you spent on it."

"That I will work to make you perform at your best."

Read the covenant to your students on the first day of classes and ask them whether they are willing to abide by it. You can certainly make it part of the syllabus, but if you prefer a more memorable option, bring copies on separate sheets. Then, after the students' approval, you will staple the sheets to the syllabi just before distributing them to your class. Either way, it is of utmost importance that you do not change the original stipulations during the course of the term.

Show no tolerance for the antics of the overbearing, the mean-spirited, and the narcissists.

A Mixed-Bag for the Road

Your students are aware of their own edge over the older generation in the handling of all things digital. The smaller the gap between their competence and yours, the more respect you will receive, and the more in control of the class you will be. Take care of disruptions of any kind right away. Interrupt your class if necessary, and allow it to continue only after the disruptive behavior is corrected. It is unfortunate that teachers are reluctant to report egregious breaches in civility and ethics because they perceive them as personal defeats, and for fear that administrators will deem them unable to control their classes. This, of course, gives students the impression that they can act with impunity, which makes them repeat their behavior. It is also unfortunate that when breaches are reported, administrators often appear reluctant to discipline a paying constituency. This wrongly reinforces the students' feeling that their transgressions will be tolerated.

Keep exceptions to the rules to a minimum. If your syllabus says "No make-up tests," explain that you really mean it out of fairness to the contingent of students respecting the rule. Place plenty of emphasis on the notion that it is not acceptable to come to class without having read and assimilated the assigned material. Help your students prepare for their tests. They will be more likely to do well, which means fewer challenges of grades. When students come to class unprepared, it does not necessarily mean that they have not opened their books. It is easy to mistake inability to study for a lukewarm interest in the subject; teach them what it means to study in earnest. Inform them that study is just another form of work. As such, it is most rewarding when you reach a state of uninterrupted absorption in what you are doing. It is the mental state called "flow." Show no tolerance for the antics of the overbearing, the mean-spirited, and the narcissists.

However, never cease to be clear-headed, temperate, considerate, and compassionate. Never argue or raise your voice. In a particularly difficult encounter with a student, imagine that you are being videotaped and that the resulting video will be used to train other teachers in the handling of such situations. While remaining engaged, you will perceive the hostility directed at you less like a personal attack and more like a management task.

There is no doubt that today's relationship between college professors and students is fraught with tension. And it is becoming clear that the massive presence of the Net in college students' lives is contributing to that tension. By casting a glance at why and how that happens, these pages are a contribution to an area of interest in which scholarly work is destined to grow in the years to come. Examining what being a teacher and a student entails is going to be an important task within the larger enterprise of reconceptualizing what being human is in the age of the Net.

14

Banning Online Comments Is Not the Answer to Online Incivility

Maria Konnikova

Maria Konnikova is a Russian-American writer and journalist who writes primarily about psychology and literature.

Some experts claim that anonymity encourages online incivility; others argue that anonymity encourages participation and promotes creativity, and still others argue that anonymous incivility is not a result of Internet technology but how human behavior changes when communication is more removed. In truth, banning online comments is not likely to reduce online incivility, as bans may simply move anonymous venom to venues such as Facebook and Twitter. Unlike online publications, these forums have no common identity, further increasing the lack of accountability among anonymous writers. Moreover, anonymous forums are often self-regulating. Indeed, people tend to discount extreme anonymous comments. In the end, research shows that those who make uncivil anonymous comments ultimately reveal themselves for what they are.

Several weeks ago, on September 24th [2013], *Popular Science* announced that it would banish comments from its Web site. The editors argued that Internet comments, particularly anonymous ones, undermine the integrity of science and lead to a culture of aggression and mockery that hinders sub-

Maria Konnikova, "The Psychology of Online Comments," *Elements* [*New Yorker* blog], October 24, 2013. © The New Yorker/Maria Konnikova/Condé Nast. Reproduced by permission.

stantive discourse. "Even a fractious minority wields enough power to skew a reader's perception of a story," wrote the online-content director Suzanne LaBarre, citing a recent study from the University of Wisconsin-Madison as evidence. While it's tempting to blame the Internet, incendiary rhetoric has long been a mainstay of public discourse. [Roman philosopher] Cicero, for one, openly called [Roman politician] Mark Antony a "public prostitute," concluding, "but let us say no more of your profligacy and debauchery." What, then, has changed with the advent of online comments?

The Impact of Anonymity

Anonymity, for one thing. According to a September Pew poll, a quarter of Internet users have posted comments anonymously. As the age of a user decreases, his reluctance to link a real name with an online remark increases; forty per cent of people in the eighteen-to-twenty-nine-year-old demographic have posted anonymously. One of the most common critiques of online comments cites a disconnect between the commenter's identity and what he is saying, a phenomenon that the psychologist John Suler memorably termed the "online disinhibition effect." The theory is that the moment you shed your identity the usual constraints on your behavior go, too—or, to rearticulate the 1993 Peter Steiner cartoon, on the Internet, nobody knows you're not a dog. When Arthur Santana, a communications professor at the University of Houston, analyzed nine hundred randomly chosen user comments on articles about immigration, half from newspapers that allowed anonymous postings, such as the *Los Angeles Times* and the *Houston Chronicle*, and half from ones that didn't, including *USA Today* and the *Wall Street Journal*, he discovered that anonymity made a perceptible difference: a full fifty-three per cent of anonymous commenters were uncivil, as opposed to twenty-nine per cent of registered, non-anonymous commenters. Anonymity, Santana concluded, encouraged incivility.

On the other hand, anonymity has also been shown to encourage participation; by promoting a greater sense of community identity, users don't have to worry about standing out individually. Anonymity can also boost a certain kind of creative thinking and lead to improvements in problem-solving. In a study that examined student learning, the psychologists Ina Blau and Avner Caspi found that, while face-to-face interactions tended to provide greater satisfaction, in anonymous settings participation and risk-taking flourished.

As personal responsibility becomes more diffused in a group, people tend to dehumanize others and become more aggressive toward them.

Anonymous forums can also be remarkably self-regulating: we tend to discount anonymous or pseudonymous comments to a much larger degree than commentary from other, more easily identifiable sources. In a 2012 study of anonymity in computer interactions, researchers found that, while anonymous comments were more likely to be contrarian and extreme than non-anonymous ones, they were also far less likely to change a subject's opinion on an ethical issue, echoing earlier results from the University of Arizona. In fact, as the Stanford computer scientist Michael Bernstein found when he analyzed the /b/ board of 4chan, an online discussion forum that has been referred to as the Internet's "rude, raunchy underbelly" and where over ninety per cent of posts are wholly anonymous, mechanisms spontaneously emerged to monitor user interactions and establish a commenter's status as more or less influential—and credible.

Examining Tone and Content

Owing to the conflicting effects of anonymity, and in response to the changing nature of online publishing itself, Internet researchers have begun shifting their focus away from anonymity toward other aspects of the online environment, such as tone and content. The University of Wisconsin-Madison study that *Popular Science* cited, for instance, was focused on whether comments themselves, anonymous or otherwise, made people less civil. The authors found that the nastier the comments, the more polarized readers became about the contents of the article, a phenomenon they dubbed the "nasty effect." But the nasty effect isn't new, or unique to the Internet. Psychologists have long worried about the difference between face-to-face communication and more removed ways of talking—the letter, the telegraph, the phone. Without the traditional trappings of personal communication, like non-verbal cues, context, and tone, comments can become overly impersonal and cold.

But a ban on article comments may simply move them to a different venue, such as Twitter or Facebook—from a community centered around a single publication or idea to one without any discernible common identity. Such large group environments, in turn, often produce less than desirable effects, including a diffusion of responsibility: you feel less accountable for your own actions, and become more likely to engage in amoral behavior. In his classic work on the role of groups and media exposure in violence, the social cognitive psychologist Alfred Bandura found that, as personal responsibility becomes more diffused in a group, people tend to dehumanize others and become more aggressive toward them. At the same time, people become more likely to justify their actions in self-absolving ways. Multiple studies have also illustrated that when people don't think they are going to be held immediately accountable for their words they are more likely to fall back on mental shortcuts in their thinking and writing, processing information less thoroughly. They become, as a result, more likely to resort to simplistic evaluations of complicated issues, as the psychologist Philip Tetlock has repeatedly found over several decades of research on accountability.

Removing comments also affects the reading experience itself: it may take away the motivation to engage with a topic more deeply, and to share it with a wider group of readers. In a phenomenon known as shared reality, our experience of something is affected by whether or not we will share it socially. Take away comments entirely, and you take away some of that shared reality, which is why we often want to share or comment in the first place. We want to believe that others will read and react to our ideas.

Whether online, on the phone, by telegraph, or in person, we are governed by the same basic principles. The medium may change, but people do not.

Social Controls

What the University of Wisconsin-Madison study may ultimately show isn't the negative power of a comment in itself but, rather, the cumulative effect of a lot of positivity or negativity in one place, a conclusion that is far less revolutionary. One of the most important controls of our behavior is the established norms within any given community. For the most part, we act consistently with the space and the situation; a football game is different from a wedding, usually. The same phenomenon may come into play in different online forums, in which the tone of existing comments and the publication itself may set the pace for a majority of subsequent interactions. [Researchers Ashley A.] Anderson, [Dominique] Brossard, and their colleagues' experiment lacks the crucial element of setting, since the researchers created fake comments on a fake post, where the tone was simply either civil or uncivil ("If you don't see the benefits . . . you're an idiot").

Would the results have been the same if the uncivil remarks were part of a string of comments on a *New York Times* article or a Gawker [gawker.com] post, where comments can be promoted or demoted by other users? On Gawker, in the process of voting a comment up or down, users can set the tone of the comments, creating a surprisingly civil result. The readership, in other words, spots the dog at the other of the end of the keyboard, and puts him down.

As the psychologists Marco Yzer and Brian Southwell put it, "new communication technologies do not fundamentally alter the theoretical bounds of human interaction; such inter-action continues to be governed by basic human tendencies." Whether online, on the phone, by telegraph, or in person, we are governed by the same basic principles. The medium may change, but people do not. The question instead is whether the outliers, the trolls and the flamers will hold outsized influ-ence—and the answer seems to be that, even protected by the shade of anonymity, a dog will often make himself known with a stray, accidental bark. Then, hopefully, he will be treated accordingly.

15

Media, Not Courts, Should Determine Anonymous Online Comment Policies

Kathy English

Kathy English, public editor for the Toronto Star, *serves on the Canadian Journalism Association Ethics Panel and the executive committee of the Canadian Journalism Foundation. As a public editor, English supervises journalism ethics, examines critical errors or omissions, and acts as public liaison for the* Toronto Star.

Growing incivility from those who lack the courage to identify themselves has online media questioning how best to deal with the challenges of anonymous comments. News media must strike a balance between addressing hateful, uniformed comments and promoting free expression. In some cases, courts have intervened and compelled media to expose the identity of anonymous online commenters who violate the rights of others. To avoid such intervention, media should take steps to encourage online commenters to reveal their identities. In the end, to maintain journalistic ethics, encourage free speech, and protect privacy, media should address anonymous online incivility so that courts do not have to do so.

"CrankyOld Fart," who are you really? And I have to ask, why do you hide behind that silly handle?

"Crazy Canuck," "EagerBeaver," "Surfer Sam," "Pretty Kitty" and all you thousands of others who post your strong views

Kathy English, "Online Anonymity and the Law," *Toronto Star* [ONT], April 17, 2010.

pseudonymously in the *Star's* online comments, I wonder: Would you be willing to express your opinions under your real names?

Can news organizations find a way to compel online commenters to speak out under their true identities? Should the media ever unmask anonymous commenters? Can the courts force them to do so? Should they?

Most importantly, is the end of online anonymity near?

Questioning Online Anonymity

These are important questions now under consideration in news organizations and courts throughout North America. This week [April 2010], a Nova Scotia judge ordered both Google and a weekly newspaper called the *Coast* to provide information about the identities of people who posted anonymous critical comments about the Halifax fire chief and his deputy.

In so doing, Justice Heather Robertson of the Nova Scotia Supreme Court ruled that people who post comments anonymously must be held accountable for their actions.

In Ottawa, a case that similarly challenges principles of privacy and freedom of expression are at stake as a panel of Divisional Court judges considers an appeal of a lower court's decision that operators of a right-wing website called freedominion.com must disclose the email and IP [Internet Protocol] addresses of eight anonymous commenters who posted disparaging comments about an Ottawa human rights lawyer.

Earlier this month, the *Cleveland Plain Dealer* sparked an industry-wide ethical debate about anonymity and online comments when it disclosed the email identity of an online commenter named "lawmiss" who criticized the paper's coverage of several controversial criminal cases and posted a personal attack that questioned the mental state of a reporter's relative.

In removing the comment because it violated the website's standards, an online editor discovered the comments came from the personal email address of the judge who was presiding over those cases.

The judge denies posting the messages and has launched a lawsuit against the *Plain Dealer* for violating her privacy. Her daughter subsequently came forward and said she had used her mother's email to post some comments.

While we . . . applaud the notion of a wired citizenry that's fully engaged with the news, we believe the conversation would be far more civil and informative if everyone spoke out under their true identities.

While the newspaper has come under some fire for exposing the commenter's email identity, the paper's editor contends that not publishing the explosive revelation would have been a violation of journalistic responsibility given the seriousness of the criminal cases the judge is presiding over.

A Spectrum of Views

Moving forward, I expect these developments will affect how news organizations handle the vexing issues related to online commenting. These challenges play out daily at the *Star*, which launched online comments nearly three years ago and now receives more than 15,000 comments each month—most of them pseudonymous.

On one hand, there are those who suggest the *Star* is stifling debate in moderating and limiting online commenting and not posting comments that violate our extensive commenting guidelines. At the other end of the spectrum are those who question why the *Star* publishes what they regard as ill-informed, mean-spirited comments from people who seemingly don't have the courage to put their names to their convictions.

Ask journalists about online commenting and you're apt to get an earful about what many of us regard as the scourge of (pseudo)-anonymity. While we have come to understand the digital reality of "news as a conversation," indeed, applaud the notion of a wired citizenry that's fully engaged with the news, we believe the conversation would be far more civil and informative if everyone spoke out under their true identities, as has traditionally been required on the Letters page.

"I look forward to the day when news organizations start to ban anonymous comments on their websites," Connie Schultz, the Cleveland newspaper's Pulitzer Prize winning columnist, wrote in a recent column that aptly expressed the views of many journalists.

"Maybe that's the foolish optimist in me, but I want to believe that we will finally admit—to ourselves and to the public at large—that allowing people to hide behind anonymity has not been good for our industry, our culture, our country."

While I second those emotions and abhor the nasty discourse of those whom I expect would temper their tone if they had to provide their names, I don't think there are easy solutions here. If we simply ban anonymous comments, how would we verify the identities of thousands of commenters?

Still, it's preferable that the media figure this out rather than the courts. Like many news organizations, the *Star* is now reviewing its online commenting policies and examining how we might encourage commenters to voluntarily reveal their true identities. One possibility being tried in some newsrooms is to give greater prominence to commenters who do speak out under their real names. Stay tuned for more on this. In the meantime: Commenters—perhaps it's time you unmask yourselves.

Organizations to Contact

The editors have compiled the following list of organizations concerned with the issues debated in this book. The descriptions are derived from materials provided by the organizations. All have publications or information available for interested readers. The list was compiled on the date of publication of the present volume; names, addresses, phone and fax numbers, and e-mail and Internet addresses may change. Be aware that many organizations take several weeks or longer to respond to inquiries, so allow as much time as possible.

American Enterprise Institute for Public Policy Research (AEI)
1150 17th St. NW, Washington, DC 20036
(202) 862-5800 • fax: (202) 862-7178
e-mail: info@aei.org
website: www.aei.org

The American Enterprise Institute for Public Policy Research (AEI) is a conservative, libertarian public policy research organization that explores economics, trade, social welfare, government spending and policy, domestic politics, defense, and foreign policy. The Institute publishes books, articles, reports, and its policy magazine, *The American*. Articles on political partisanship and incivility are available on its website, including "Poisonous Political Atmosphere Is Unhealthy" and "A Nation Closely Divided, Not Dangerously Polarized."

Brookings Institution
1775 Massachusetts Ave. NW, Washington, DC 20036
(202) 797-6000 • fax: (202) 797-6004
e-mail: communications@brookings.edu
website: www.brookings.edu

Founded in 1927, the Brookings Institution is a public policy think tank that studies a broad range of issues that impact the United States domestically and internationally. It publishes the quarterly *Brookings Review*, as well as numerous books and research papers. Institution resources on political partisanship and incivility available on its website include "Red and Blue Nation: How Deep is America's Political Divide?" and "Make US Politics Safe for Moderates."

Cato Institute

1000 Massachusetts Ave. NW, Washington, DC   20001-5403
(202) 842-0200 • fax: (202) 842-3490
website: www.cato.org

Cato Institute is a libertarian public policy research foundation dedicated to limited government and support of the free market. It generally opposes any restrictions on free speech, including those that some might consider uncivil. It publishes numerous reports, analysis, commentary, and the periodicals *Policy Analysis* and *Cato Policy Review*. Resources on political partisanship and incivility are available on its website, including "Responses on Political Theory, Idealism, and Extremism" and "In Class War, It's the 'Middle' Ground that's Key."

Center for Information and Research on Civic Learning and Engagement (CIRCLE)

Jonathan M. Tisch College of Citizenship and Public Service
Lincoln Filene Hall, Tufts University, Medford, MA   02155
(617) 627-4710 • fax: (617) 627-3401
e-mail: civicyouth@tufts.edu
website: www.civicyouth.org

Since 2001, the Center for Information and Research on Civic Learning and Engagement (CIRCLE) has been conducting research focused on the civic engagement of American youth from their education to their political participation. With the development of research in this field, the Center has influenced the discussion about the young generation of citizens, encouraged politics to include these citizens in political campaigns, and helped train organizations on how to reach young Americans. CIRCLE studies a wide range of topics including civic knowledge, concepts of citizenship, and civic education. Findings and reports available on the CIRCLE website include "Youth Attitudes Toward Civility in Politics."

The Century Foundation (TCF)
41 E. 70th St., New York, NY   10021
(212) 535-4441 • fax: (212) 879-9197
website: http://tcf.org

The Century Foundation (TCF) is a nonprofit public policy research institution committed to effective government, open democracy, and competitive markets. One major concern of TCF is the impact of media on the public. Foundation-published resources on this issue explore media criticism and youth political engagement. Recent commentaries in this topic area include "Social Media in This Age of Turmoil" and "The Future of News."

Deliberative Democracy Consortium (DDC)
1050 17th St., Suite 250, Washington, DC   20036
website: www.deliberative-democracy.net

The mission of the Deliberative Democracy Consortium (DDC) is to bring together practitioners and researchers to support and foster the growing movement to promote and institutionalize deliberative democracy at all levels of governance in the United States and worldwide. The *Journal of Public Deliberation* is a collaboration between the DDC and the International Association for Public Participation (IAP2). DDC articles, reports, and blog entries can be found on its website.

Institute for Civility in Government (ICG)
PO Box 41804, Houston, TX   77241-1804
(713) 444-1254
e-mail: info@instituteforcivility.org
website: www.instituteforcivility.org

Believing that a lack of participation and growing polarization along lines of race, class, religion, age, and ideology pose a serious threat to the nation, the Institute for Civility in Government (ICG) seeks to reduce the polarization of the nation's political and legislative processes by facilitating dialogue, teaching respect, and building civility in both the public and private spheres. The Institute hosts civility training workshops, forums, and seminars and publishes *Reclaiming Civility in the Public Square*. Resources on civility can be found on ICG's *Civility Blog* and its website's civility reading list.

National Civility Center

119 W. Mississippi Dr., Suite 3, Muscatine, IA   52761
website: www.civilitycenter.org

Established in 2000, the National Civility Center believes that a comprehensive approach to community improvement that engages all local stakeholders around shared ideas and a unified plan for action can help community members and organizations become more effective at solving tough social issues. The Center publishes *Bring a Dish to Pass: The Civil Action of Community Improvement* to be used as a tool to promote community dialogue.

National Constitution Center

Independence Mall, 525 Arch St., Philadelphia, PA   19106
(215) 409-6600
website: http://constitutioncenter.org

The National Constitution Center illuminates constitutional ideals and inspires active citizenship through a museum experience that includes interactive exhibits, films, and rare artifacts. The Center also provides a forum for constitutional dialogue, engaging diverse and distinguished leaders of government, public policy, journalism, and scholarship in public discussion and debate. On its website's Civility and Democracy link, the Center provides access to resources from its interdisciplinary forum titled *Can We Talk? A Conversation about Civility and Democracy in America*. The forum offers a view of the current state of public discourse and the issue of civility in the context of the roles that dissent and protest play in American politics.

National Education Association (NEA)

1201 16th St. NW, Washington, DC   20036-3290
(202) 833-4000 • fax: (202) 822-7974
website: www.nea.org

The National Education Association (NEA) works to ensure that all American children have access to a quality public education. Its focus ranges from large legislative matters to school policy level issues, including technology and classroom management. Articles that deal with technology in the classroom and classroom civility can be found on its website, including "Desperately Seeking Civility" and "Classroom Civility: Is It Just Me?"

Reason Foundation

3415 S. Sepulveda Blvd., Suite 400, Los Angeles, CA   90034
(310) 391-2245 • fax: (310) 391-4395
website: www.reason.org

The Reason Foundation promotes free-market principles and opposes restrictions of free speech. On its website, the Foundation publishes newsletters, testimony, court briefs, policy studies, and commentary by policy experts and articles from the monthly *Reason* magazine, including "Political Discourse and the Tucson Shootings: Is This a Teachable Moment?" and "This 'Conversation' Is a Set-Up: Political Rhetoric Is Not the Problem."

Bibliography

Books

Sunil Ahuja   *Congress Behaving Badly: The Rise of Partisanship and Incivility and the Death of Public Trust.* Westport, CT: Praeger, 2008.

Elijah Anderson   *The Cosmopolitan Canopy: Race and Civility in Everyday Life.* New York: W.W. Norton, 2011.

Jeffrey M. Berry and Sarah Sobieraj   *The Outrage Industry: Political Opinion Media and the New Incivility.* New York: Oxford University Press, 2013.

Cornell W. Clayton and Richard Elgar, eds.   *Civility and Democracy in America: A Reasonable Understanding.* Pullman, WA: Washington State University Press, 2012.

Cassandra Dahnke, Thomas Spath, and Donna Bowling   *Reclaiming Civility in the Public Square: 10 Rules That Work.* Livermore, CA: WingSpan Press, 2007.

Marcus Leonard Daniel   *Scandal & Civility: Journalism and the Birth of American Democracy.* New York: Oxford University Press, 2009.

P.M. Forni   *Choosing Civility: The Twenty-Five Rules of Considerate Conduct.* New York: Macmillan, 2010.

Lawrence J.
Friedman and
Mark D.
McGarvie, eds.

Charity, Philanthropy, and Civility in American History. New York: Cambridge University Press, 2003.

Susan Herbert

Rude Democracy: Civility and Incivility in American Politics. Philadelphia: Temple University Press, 2010.

Mark Kingwell

Unruly Voices: Essays on Democracy, Civility, and the Human Imagination. Emeryville, Ontario, Canada: Biblioasis, 2012.

Parker J. Palmer

Healing the Heart of Democracy: The Courage to Create a Politics Worthy of the Human Spirit. San Francisco: Jossey-Bass, 2011.

Christine Pearson
and Christine
Porath

The Cost of Bad Behavior. New York: Penguin, 2009.

Phillip Smith,
Timothy L.
Phillips, and Ryan
D. King

Incivility: The Rude Stranger in Everyday Life. New York: Cambridge University Press, 2010.

Bill Stumpf

The Ice Palace That Melted Away: Restoring Civility and Other Lost Virtues to Everyday Life. New York: Pantheon, 1998.

Terri Jo Swim,
Keith Howard,
and Il-Hee Kim,
eds.

The Hope for Audacity: Recapturing Optimism and Civility in Education. New York: Peter Lang, 2012.

Darla J. Twale and Barbara M. De Luca — *Faculty Incivility: The Rise of the Academic Bully Culture and What to Do About It.* San Francisco: Jossey-Bass, 2008.

Jean M. Twenge and W. Keith Campbell — *The Narcissism Epidemic: Living in the Age of Entitlement.* New York: Free Press, 2009.

Periodicals and Internet Sources

A.A. Anderson et al. — "The 'Nasty Effect': Online Incivility and Risk Perceptions of Emerging Technologies," *Journal of Computer-Mediated Communication,* 2013.

John M. Buchanan — "How to Disagree," *Christian Century,* November 13, 2013.

Stanley Crouch — "For Love of Money and Fear of Truth," *New York Daily News,* November 8, 2010.

Leah Eichler — "Sorry to Be Rude, but My Phone Needs Me," *Globe and Mail,* October 5, 2013.

Linda Feldmann — "Why People Feel Free to Heckle President Obama," *Christian Science Monitor,* November 30, 2013.

Jason Flom — "Breeding Civility with Civility," *Q.E.D.,* March 3, 2013. http://qedfoundation.org.

John F. Gaski — "Positive Effects of Negative Political Ads," *Washington Times,* November 1, 2010.

Marilyn Gilroy — "College Grappling with Incivility," *The Hispanic Outlook in Higher Education*, June 30, 2008.

Glenn Greenwald — "Journalists Angry Over the Commission of Journalism," *Salon*, February 14, 2011. www.salon.com.

David Greisman — "How Civil Are We?," *Carroll Magazine*, April 1, 2012. www.carrollmagazine.com.

M.E. Kabay — "See You Anon: Reflections on Online Anonymity," *Network World*, September 26, 2011. www.networkworld.com.

Jack Knox — "An Epidemic of Incivility in the Age of Anonymity," *Times Colonist*, January 14, 2011.

Mike Littwin — "Incivility Debate Goes Beyond Words," *Denver Post*, January 13, 2011.

Vinay Menon — "We Are Living in an Age of Nastiness, Deceit and Malice," *Toronto Star*, November 16, 2013.

Mark Milke — "The Decline in Civility Can Be Traced Back to Ted Kennedy," *Calgary Herald*, March 6, 2011.

Susan Perry — "Trolls, Spambots, and the Psychology of Online Comments," MinnPost, October 28, 2013. www.minnpost.com.

Peter Post   "Technology and Stress Are Making
                    Us Ruder," *Boston Globe*, October 27,
                    2013.

Gillian Shaw   "Is Social Media Making Us Rude?,"
                    Star Phoenix, October 26, 2013.

Anne Springer   "Celebrities' Recent Lack of Civility
                    Raises Role Model Questions,"
                    Gloucester Times, September 23, 2009.

Neil Steinberg   "Land of the Free, Home of the
                    Skeptic," *Chicago Sun-Times*, April 21,
                    2010.

Alina Tugend   "Incivility Can Have Costs Beyond
                    Hurt Feelings," *New York Times*,
                    November 19, 2010.

Linton Weeks   "Please Read This Story, Thank You,"
                    NPR, March 14, 2012. www.npr.org.

Michael R. Wolf,   "Incivility and Standing Firm: A
J. Cherie   Second Layer of Partisan Division,"
Strachan, and   *Political Science & Policies*, July 2012.
Daniel M. Shea

Don   "Incivility May Be Down, but
Wolfensberger   'Uncivility' Persists," *Roll Call*, June 5,
                    2012. www.rollcall.com.

Index